THE GHOST IN THE ORA]

THE GHOST IN THE ORANGE CLOSET©

Facing Wounds You Can't See

War Veterans' Trek Beyond Post Traumatic Stress Disorder

Manufactured in the United States of America

Published by TLV Investments LLC

Co-editor: M K Destro

Printing by: MIRA

Library of Congress Cataloging-in-Publication Data

Criser, TL,

The Ghost in the Orange Closet/ TL Criser

1. Vietnam, PDST—Non Fiction 2. 1st Cavalry—Vietnam

3. Post Traumatic Stress Disorder

THREAD ID: (1-1GW5PY)

ISBN 978-0-9820519-0-0

Acknowledgements

To Leslie for her determination that this book be written. To Mindy & James Destro, Patricia Holloway, Irish John and Sue Gore, Rosanne and Dr. William Milroy, Neal & Linda Kusumoto, and Billie and Jim Hartless for their contribution, encouragement, patience, and assistance. To Walker Jones...and the brothers and sisters of the 1st of the 9th Cavalry for their friendship. And, last but most certainly not least, to Peggy Matern for the opportunity to build on my writing skills.

Cover Photo: Returning from a mission are (left to right) Lt. Glenn A. (Buddha) Jenkins, Sgt. Richard Dornellas, and the author Tom Criser share a few laughs. Other names not available. Date: June 1969

Author's note: A portion of any author royalties earned from the sale of this book will go to military support organizations such as the USO, Wounded Warriors, Veteran's of Foreign Wars, and others.

Dedication

To Those Who
Unselfishly Serve
To
Protect Others.

To Those Who
Silently Scream
From
Unseen Wounds

To Those Who
Go Flag Draped
To
Fiddler's Green

About The Author

Tom Criser is the Author of "A Little Beggar's Shoes" an adventure tale of young rascals living in Post WWII Germany, and he co-authored "Doctors Are From Jupiter" a medical coding and compliance book, co-authored by Trey Dunaway, MD and Former OIG Criminal Investigator, Joe Batte, CPE.

Mr. Criser spent more than 20 years writing radio and television commercials, newsletters, and marketing material. He is the owner of TLV Investments formerly known as TLC Advertising.

He served in Vietnam in 1969 and 1970 with the Blue Annihilators of C Troop, 1st Squadron, 9th Cavalry a division of the 1st Airmobile Cavalry.

Contents

Introduction

In researching this book, I found more than 658,000 Google hits on Vietnam and Post Traumatic Stress Disorder (PTSD). Looking further, I found numerous books on Vietnam and more than 450,000 hits on books and papers written about PTSD. With those numbers, a friend questioned the need for another book and wondered what would be different about this book.

Great question! It made me think for some time, years to be exact, to find the answer. Some of the most helpful data I found in looking at books about this topic are the reader reviews. The question I honestly found most often was, "*Is this another story about the horrors of war, heroes, firefights, and how we could have won the war?*"

The answer is both yes and no. It is about heroes, but those heroes who never "ever" thought of themselves as such. "*We were just doing a job,*" is what I hear from so many Vets today.

Is it about firefights and the horrors of war? Yes, in part. You do have to establish enduring characters to make someone believe they were heroes. You also have to describe the horrors of war to show that Post Traumatic Stress Disorder (PTSD) often results as "unseen wounds of war."

This brings up the second most covered topic in the book reviews, "*what qualifies the author to write this book?*" Boy, this was the question I had the most difficult time answering. Yes, I was with one of the most active and most decorated Helicopter Attack units in the war. Yes, I was in more than 200 combat assaults. Yes, I lost comrades-in-arms. But, does that make me an authority? No…just experienced!

Do I believe I was a hero? That's a gigantic NO! I'm like the rest…I was doing a job. "*I was drafted and wanted nothing more than serve my country and get the Puck out of Dodge!*" I've stated that many times and most veterans respond, "*So was I …so did I, but I would use the F word!*"

And while we're thinking about words, let's think about the word… Vietnam! There really is no other idiom in the American language that evokes raw emotions like the word "Vietnam." That's predominantly the case for those who lived through the war years 1965 to 1975. And it doesn't matter whether they were part of the millions who expressed their rights of Freedom of Speech and marched in peace rallies...or the 3.1 million who fought for the rights of Freedom of Speech and served in our military.

Sadly, the most vivid memory of the war ending, for most Americans, is watching news clips of the American Embassy filled with pleading Vietnamese who had climbed to the rooftop as our helicopters evacuated the last of our people. Or it's the scene of UH-1 helicopters, the workhorse of our military, recklessly shoved off the decks of our warships to make room for others flying in with a full load of evacuees.

Millions found it more palatable to subdue those memories of our ignominious retreat and just try to move on. However, those memories are now brought to the forefront by the current war and are mushrooming clouds seeking a resolution.

What makes the United States of America such an amazing and magnificent place is the optimistic, entrepreneurial, and speculative nature of its people. Those who migrated to this country were risk takers. It took enormous courage to risk leaving behind a familiar environment and people you love to move to a foreign land. Or to undertake an even more awesome risk by bringing an entire family, for whom you're responsible, across a treacherous 3,000-mile ocean to get to this country.

Whether there is a gene in those who are risk takers or it's a special personality trait, those who ventured here passed on the courageous and speculative characteristics to their children and grandchildren. And that distinctive American persona, combined with our military's renowned attitude and dedication to "leave no man behind" in the battlefield, will not let us file away the Vietnam war. We must face our fears and acknowledge our defeats rather than pretending they didn't exist and locking our "Ghosts" into a closet somewhere in the back of our minds.

And the last question: "*How is this book different?*" The answer came through our 1st of the 9th Cavalry chatgroup and the communications we have had over the last eight years. The perception and significance of the Vietnam War has changed. That era is now at last approaching a satisfactory resolution for those who lived through it, had relatives lost in it, and as part of the history of the United States of America.

Finally...value is being extracted out of our Vietnam experience. The time has come to discharge the "Ghosts in our Closets" so we can, at long last, put it to rest and, more importantly, prevent The Ghosts of "Traumatic Stress" from being buried in the minds of our soldiers of today. That's what this book is all about.

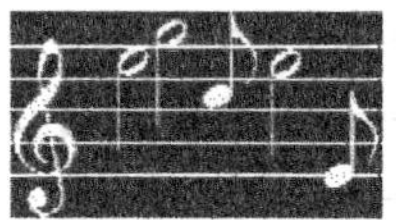

LATE AT NIGHT WHILE YOU'RE SLEEPING

Chapter I – The Ghost: A Vietnam Soldier's Legacy

In the deepest recesses of your mind is a hiding place…a closet to put old things. You don't really know it's there, nor do you know when something goes in. At times it took seconds…or minutes…or hours to fill it. When the time came and the closet became full, we closed the door tightly, hoping to never have to look inside again.

At first, The Ghost inside that closet rattled and raged wanting to be let out. But, we resisted, we pushed it deeper and deeper until we couldn't hear it any more. The closet, and what was in it, was forgotten. We lived our lives, in most cases quite successfully, never thinking about it again.

Ten, twenty, and more years passed. And somehow the closet prisoner makes changes in you without you ever knowing the changes are taking place. Others around you see the changes quite clearly. Most say nothing, because even to them the changes are slow and acceptable. They love you and don't want to hurt you or your feelings.

Years later there is that one day when you look in the mirror and what you see is a shadow of your old self. The weight of what you pushed into the closet was much more than you ever imagined. Then, in one sudden moment…one split second…the closet opens and the mirror image you see is The Ghost. The Ghost stares you in the face! It shakes you to the core of your soul.

For some, there is only one answer…end it all. Others seek help in the wrong places, a bottle or drugs, and only postpone the inevitable.

For me, help came just in time from the right places and the right people. It came in an 8 ½ by 11 inch white envelope. It looked just like another piece of junk mail. But there was something in the top left hand corner. It was something I had not seen in 19 years, or when I did see it I quickly looked the other way. Not this time!

It was a yellow shield, round at the top, and coming to a rounded point at the bottom. A black border caressed the outside. Across the center slanted from left to right was a black line and in the top of the right side was a black head of a horse. It was the 1st Cavalry Patch. The lettering below said, "C Troop 1/9th Cav."

I didn't dismiss it like I had in the past, since years before a friend had handed me a newsletter from the Army's 1st Cavalry Division. The friend, Dale Rickards, was in the Cav during World War II when some of them actually still rode horses.

Dale, a fellow Kiwanian, had heard I was in the 1st Cav during Vietnam and thought I would be interested. I took the newsletter and put it into my desk drawer. Each time I opened that drawer I thought maybe I should read it and see if it mentioned Charlie Troop, 1st Squadron 9th Cavalry, a division of the 1st (Airmobile) Cavalry. But time passed swiftly…five years to be exact.

The arrival of the white envelope seemed to come magically when I finally was resolved to read the newsletter. One morning, in the spring of 1999, I pulled the newsletter from under several files that now covered it and put it on top of the inbox hoping to find some time that day to scan through it.

The white envelope arrived in the mail that day. It contained a welcoming note from a former Charlie Trooper, Walker Jones, whose call-sign in Vietnam was Cavalier 25, and a list of names from my unit from 1965 to 1972.

In the years since 1970, when I returned home, there were a few occasions when I permitted myself to think about Vietnam. Each time I did...it ended with disastrous results. Nightmares for months, migraine headaches, depression, and general irritation making me feel nothing could make me happy again.

Ten years after coming back, I went through one such incident. I went to see the movie, "Apocalypse Now." I was told it was a great movie about Vietnam with Marlon Brando, Robert Duval, and Martin Sheen, all great actors. However, when I saw the helicopter scene and the yellow circles on the doors of the choppers, I had to walk out. Those were our choppers! It was Charlie Troop who had circles on their doors. It was the Blue Platoon who hung out of the birds as they went in for landings. It was our officers who wore the Stetson.

The Ghost in my closet hammered to come out, but I wasn't ready. I wasn't prepared to deal with those raw emotions, which make you feel like you're losing control with your hands and knees shaking chaotically.

A friend suggested writing down the emotions I felt to possibly find relief. I sat down and tried to write what I felt, but nothing came. Then, I realized I really didn't remember much about my 412 days in Vietnam with the Blue Annihilators. I couldn't remember many of the places, names, or why we were there. I had successfully suppressed the memories. And that is what I ended up writing.

Vietnam Remembered

I can't remember most of the names
and all the faces are a darkened blur.
I can't remember all the strange places,
but the smell of death is forever there.

I can't remember the empty laughter
or the jokes we told to ease our minds.
I can't remember why we were all there,
but the fear takes me clearly back at times.

I can't remember the Sunday I turned 22,
but I think I killed a shadowy enemy that day.
I can't remember why I shouted,
"He's still alive" when my friend's last breath passed away.

I can't remember the hootchmaid's name
who read in our cards who was to die.

I can't remember why we nervously laughed,
but my nightmares know she didn't lie.

I can't remember the FNG who stood in my place*
while my R & R took me on an Australian high.
I can't remember the number of tears I spent...
when I heard it was he who took my place to die.

I can remember yesterday my son asking me,
while dressed in green with his toy gun.
I can remember the gleam of excitement in his eyes,
"Dad, was getting those medals in Vietnam fun?"

(*FNG – Funny New Guy or F---ing New Guy)

It was a relief to write about it, but it also was discomforting to think I couldn't remember more. I looked through my old scrapbook and realized I only knew most of the guys by last name, or a handle they had picked up. I was known as Blue-India, the radio-telephone-operator (RTO) of the platoon from May 1969 to February 1970. Surely most of the Vietnam Vets had the same memory problems, and if they remembered me it was by my call-sign.

Since writing about Nam was somewhat helpful, I sat down and tried to write more about the emotions I felt.

Safe Return?

I busy my body past exhaustion and fill my mind with determined caution,
showing warning signs so clear,
but only to those who returned without a cheer.
Whoever sees me in my daily life isn't aware I mask those months of strife.
Though they know I fought the Asian War...little do they see the angst
pushing open the padded door. It's been a struggle through the years
with troubled times so severe...my strength can't help but quickly disappear
and let this burden overtake my tired mind,

just as the seconds there crept hours at a time.
No wounds were suffered of the flesh,
but the mind returned in a tangled mesh.
Slowly, it unwinds its haunting past;
as despair, suppressed by the years, reacts;
putting unstable emotions where I tread,
ending nightmares in screams and sweat.
I'll be alright they say and lucky to have made it through,
only wondering at times,
if the returning dead weren't lucky too.

The result was frightening. I slammed the closet door...nailed it shut, and did my best to forget the closet even existed.

In all honesty, the media had successfully made Vietnam Veterans appear psychopathic, downtrodden, homeless guys with drug or alcohol problems. And the image, I thought, wasn't helped when Vietnam Veterans walked in parades in camouflage fatigues, long scraggly beards, and sun beaten look.

At that time, I lived in Thousand Oaks, California, formerly the training camp of the Dallas Cowboys and now, at the Sherwood Country Club, the home of the Target World Challenge sponsored by The Tiger Woods Learning Center. Our Kiwanis Club was in charge of the annual Conejo Valley Days Parade held in late April. During the late 1980s and early 1990s there normally were about 180 to 200 entrants in the parade, making it one of the larger spectacles on the West Coast. My wife, Leslie, and I were in charge of managing a fleet of cars used by VIPS; mostly celebrities and politicians.

Our job, characteristically, was working through chaos and madness before the parade to make sure we had available vehicles and drivers to ferry the VIPs. Naturally, there was always a mix-up; either we had VIPs not showing up or one showing up unexpectedly. Volunteer drivers, who needed to be there at 6:30 am, had a habit of showing up late or not at all. Things typically worked out and when the parade started we actually had time to watch it.

"*Hey, look a group of Vietnam Veterans,*" my wife said, when she noticed five guys dressed in camouflage fatigues and Booney hats in the parade. They carried the black and white POW flag, a U.S. flag, and one I now have in my study, "Our Cause Was Just" flag.

"*You should be in there with them,*" she said with pride.

"*No way! That's not me!*" I told her. And it wasn't me. I wasn't a bearded homeless guy who looked like he just came out of rehab. I was truly embarrassed to be considered a Vietnam Vet.

"*But why not, you fought there, you should be proud of that,*" she said with conviction and assurance.

"*Do I look like that?*" I asked her.

"*No, but you should be proud of your service.*"

I knew she was right! But I wasn't ready to let my ghost out of the closet.

Many years later she did, however, convince me to go see the moving Vietnam Wall, which was being displayed in Westlake Village, just a few miles away.

We went on a Sunday afternoon, accompanied by my two children who were 10 and 12, and took a look. I thought it would do me some good and possibly, with the support of my wife and children, I could make it without completely cracking up.

It didn't work! Nightmares, sleepless nights, and uncontrollable shaking followed for weeks. What really made things worse was my inability to remember the names of those in my platoon who died while I was there. It was astounding to me that names I should remember…names I should honor for the rest of my life…were gone.

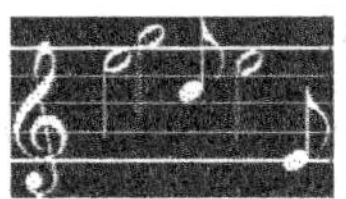

CHARLIE KONG COMES A CREEPIN ALL AROUND

Chapter II – Going To Nam

Going to Southeast Asia to fight communism didn't seem real! It was more like it was part of a movie or something you read in a book. Maybe it was because I grew up several blocks from Paramount and other Hollywood studios.

The kids on our street, Van Ness Avenue, had a choice of High Schools they could attend. I wanted to go to Hollywood High School. Except my parents, who had looked at the academic standings of schools, sent me to Fairfax High. Boy was that a mistake. Numerous kids with 4.0 grade point averages taking pre-college classes and me, who tried his best to reduce that average.

Even at Fairfax the halls echoed with names like Mickey Rooney, David Jannsen, Herb Albert, and others. Plus, the children of many actors, musicians, movie directors, and those who worked at the studios attended Fairfax. I'm sure today's students chatter about walking the same halls as Jermaine Jackson and actress Demi Moore.

Or maybe my surreal perception was because my first part-time job in high school was working around movie stars. The job was delivering stuff for The Staircase, an interior-decorating store on Melrose Place in West Los Angeles. To the customers they were "prized antique" décor items, but to me it was just stuff somebody else didn't want.

It was partially owned by the wife of George Axelrod, writer/ producer/director of movies like "Lord Love a Duck" (1965), a quirky lampoon of Southern California lifestyles, which he wrote, produced and directed. Axelrod also had success adapting the works of other writers for the movies, "Bus Stop" (1956), "Breakfast at Tiffany's" (1961) and "The Manchurian Candidate" (1962). He was responsible for the movie, "Up the Down Staircase," hence the name of the store.

I did get to meet people like Steve McQueen, Natalie Wood, Jack Lemon, Angie Dickerson, and on and on. Jack Lemon received a special delivery of an antique French desk at his studio. I remember having difficulty getting the desk through his somewhat narrow office doors. Mr. Lemon came out, helped me pick up the desk and maneuver it into his office. He was anxiously awaiting the delivery and genuinely thrilled it finally arrived.

He signed the $2,400.00 delivery invoice, had me help him move some of the furniture the way he wanted it, and gave me a $10 tip. I was very embarrassed at the price since I had just picked it up from an antique dealer for $350.00. It was my first lesson in "*Those who can afford things never think about the price. And those who know it make a hefty profit.*"

On several occasions I had to deliver items to Mr. Axelrod's home in Bel Air and to his Malibu beach house. The beach house was on Pacific Coast Highway just before you come into Malibu. It looked small from the street and, since they are jammed together with little room in between, they looked more like condominiums than houses. That was, until you walked through the rather ornate front door.

The house was wide open with imposing windows from floor to ceiling. It was laid out in a "U" shape that surrounded a rather large swimming pool. Behind a six-foot masonry wall and wrought iron gate was the sandy beach and a majestic Pacific Ocean view.

During one delivery, he was sitting by the pool reading a manuscript and drinking a beer. It appeared he just got out of the pool and was letting the afternoon sun dry him off. He offered me a beer, which I gladly accepted, and we had some conversations about German beer, surfing, and movies.

"*Aren't you a little young to know about that strong German beer?*" he asked me.

"*I was born in Germany...you can drink beer at any age if your parents are with you.*"

"*Where in Germany?*"

"*Wiesbaden, by the Rhine River.*" I explained

"*Yes, I know it well, Die Spielbank. I left some money there once,*" he said with a smile. "*And I've read The Gambler By Fyodor Dostoevsky.*"

"Yes, my mother tried to make me read it in German, but my German is just not that good anymore."

"So, you're German?"

"Half German, my father was an American GI."

He wanted to know what I wanted to do after high school and I told him I was interested in journalism.

"It's a good field to be in," I remember him saying, *"That's how I started."*

Little did I know who he really was and the extent of his involvement with such great films. To me he was the husband of Mrs. Axelrod, one of my bosses. You can imagine my surprise many years later when I found out his stature in the film industry. I thought he was just a pleasant guy who had a very nice wife.

So, like many who lived in the "tinsel-town" setting, I had a weird outlook. Until several years after I returned, my entire Vietnam experience never seemed like it was for real.

I received my draft notice in April 1968 and never doubted a trip to Southeast Asia was ahead. Growing up as an Air Force brat, my dad was a Colonel, made the appeal of a long stay in the military extremely distasteful. Even the offer to go to Officers Candidate School (OCS) I nixed, because it had a four-year hitch attached to it. Going to OCS would have delayed my departure for the jungles for several months, possibly even a year. But it was already common knowledge that officers were the number one targets and the average tour of a 1st Lieutenant was about 10 minutes after setting foot in Nam.

I stepped off the plane in Saigon on Thursday, February 13, 1969, and smelled the humid air congested with an odor of gunpowder, military machinery, and an unknown stench I learned to hate. Some said it was the smell from the human fertilizer the Vietnamese were rumored to be using. Others said it was the smell of "Crispy Critters," a term I had never heard before. Even at that, I still didn't feel this really was happening. My orders directed me to the 1st Cavalry in the Central Highlands, but first there was a brief disciplinary two week stay in Saigon.

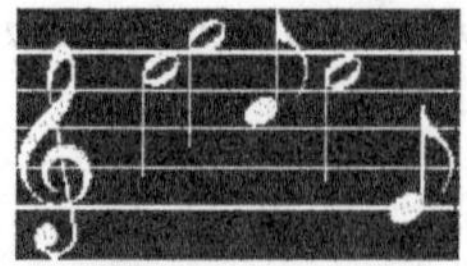

YOU'RE GONNA NEED AN OCEAN OF MOSQUITO LOTION

Chapter III – The Blue Annihilators

The 1st Airmobile Calvary arrived in Nam in 1965 and was involved in some pretty perilous missions in places like the Tranh Valley, Plaiku, and An Kha. The rather famous 7th Cavalry (Custer's Last Stand) lost half their men in battles fought in the Central Highlands. Those early years served as great lessons for how the war would be fought and how it could be won. By 1969, the 1st Cav was a skilled helicopter attack unit and a tough fighting force feared by the enemy.

It was rumored our pilots carried bounties on their heads that could have made an NVA soldier rich. The other rumor, told to us while in basic training by our Drill Instructors, was that the enemy likes to capture F----ng New Guys (FNGs) as comic relief for their troops.

At this point, the Cav was assigned to stop the North Vietnamese from coming in through Cambodia and attacking Ben Hoa and Saigon to the southeast. The 1st Squadron 9th Cavalry, one of the most decorated units in Nam, had developed into a very effective and efficient jungle warfare fighting machine and, in essence, had developed its own character.

The Commissioned and Warrant Officers, barely 20 years old, had taken the lead from an early 7st Cav Company Commander who wore a blue Stetson Hat just as he was characterized in the movie by Robert Duval. It would not have surprised anyone in the unit that one of them didn't come up with the phrase, "Love the smell of napalm in the morning." Over fifty percent of the enemy Killed In Action (KIA) by the 1st Cavalry Division was credited to the 1/9th.

Our platoon was called the Blue Annihilators; part of C Troop, 1/9th. The platoon's duty was to scout for the enemy on the ground after our reconnaissance helicopters found signs of enemy movement. If they found fresh trails, we would go in to investigate and establish if those nasty little buggers were still in the area.

The second aspect was to respond to "Downed Bird" emergencies. We responded first to rescue the crews from any downed helicopters or any fixed wing airplanes in our area. Admittedly, the call of "Downed Bird" created an incredible adrenaline high in all of us. Our actions, to do what ever was necessary to help get our guys out of trouble, were taken with hopeful and reckless abandonment. Fortunately, with vast air support, the North Vietnamese Army (NVA's) usually stayed out of sight until we were gone. Unfortunately, we mostly brought back depressing and disheartening bodybags.

The Blue Platoon never was at a full complement. The Army Manual says there should be eight to 10 men in a squad and four squads to the platoon. We were lucky to have three squads and usually only five to seven in a squad. Then, when you exclude those who had perimeter guard duty the night before and those assigned to KP, we were lucky to field two squads for any action. On some "Downed Bird" missions we only had six or seven guys…just enough to fill one Huey.

The platoon leader was called Cavalier Blue, who generally was a pilot assigned to ground duty because he raised his hand at the wrong time. It was rare any pilot would actually volunteer to be Blue, since the life expectancy was short, to say the least. I was his RTO with the call sign "Blue -India."

The roguish characteristics of the pilots carried over to the Blues who now had the look, feel, and smell of jungle fighters. Mexican Bandito style, we had bandoliers of M-60 machine gun ammo draped over the shoulders, grenades and flares on belts, and ammo packs filled with more than 200 M-16 rounds. That was all we carried; except for a canteen of water.

The Cav had learned, from years of fighting in the jungle, that strong firepower was needed to overcome the most damaging attack, an ambush. And firepower the Blues had. Besides having two M-60 machine gunners along, we had one man carry an M-79 grenade launcher and a Light Antitank

Weapon (LAW), which was great for destroying bunkers. The rest carried as much ammo we felt comfortable with.

By mid 1969, the Blues stopped utilizing the weighty helmets, which prevented you from hearing movement in the jungle, and just made noise for the enemy to hear. The Army had issued flack-jackets (bullet proof vests) and only a couple of guys wore them, due to the heat, mostly without a shirt. For the most part, we put them in our bunks in case we had to dive under them during the repeated rocket or mortar attacks. They were also good to sit on while on guard duty; it kept the ground from getting you wet.

In addition to the hefty firepower, we always had at least one Scout Bird and one Gunship (Cobra) flying close in the area. When they ran out of ammo, they hooked us up with Air Force or Navy Jets to come in and drop some heavy armament on enemy locations we designated. There also was a nearby artillery unit that our air team could bring within 20 to 30 yards of our position.

Our feeling was we were lucky. We had dry hootches to live in, somewhat comfortable cots, food served at a table, and we could shower as often as we liked. To prevent the enemy from smelling us, we used no aftershave and unscented soap. The Blues carried no heavy packs since it was a rare occasion we would be out overnight. When we got hungry and were stuck out in the field, our choppers went back for food and water. If we were in an extended firefight, our pilots and their crews would risk everything to bring us more ammunition.

As a unit we were close, trusted each other, and quickly learned our strength was rapidly assessing our enemy and then adapting to make the best of any situation. We regularly had time to relax and play sports, which made us even closer. There was a great deal of respect for each other and immense sense of pride in being part of the 1st Cavalry. Most of all, the Blues believed the true heroes of the war were the guys in the mud and jungle for months at a time and those "courageous men in their flying machines."

1/9th UNIT REPORT

On 15 September, 1965, the 1st Squadron, 9th Cavalry began combat operations in the Republic of Vietnam as the division's air cavalry squadron. The 1st Squadron, 9th Cavalry participated in such pivotal battles as the Ia Drang Valley, Khe Sahn, Binh Dinh, and QuangTri. Until 28 June 1971, the 1st Squadron, 9th Cavalry remained in Vietnam. During that period, elements from the 1st Squadron, 9th Cavalry earned fourteen campaign streamers, three Presidential Unit Citations, five Valorous Unit Citations, and the reputation as one of the finest combat units in Vietnam. It is estimated that the 1st Squadron, 9th Cavalry was responsible for fifty percent of all enemy soldiers killed by the 1st Cavalry Division during the war. It was for this reason that the battalion earned its current nickname "The Headhunters." The 1st Squadron, 9th Cavalry troopers earned two Medals of Honor in Vietnam. Hollywood honored the squadron in its fictional portrayal of an attack on a communist base camp in the film "Apocalypse Now." http://www.globalsecurity.org/military/agency/army/1-9cav.htm

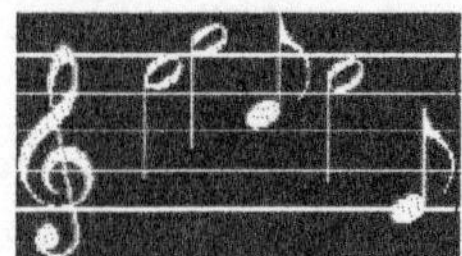

YOU'LL BE SCRATCHING LIKE A HOUND

Chapter IV – Meeting on the Net

Of course, after receiving the white envelope and an invitation to meet fellow Cavaliers on the Net, I joined the chatroom (ctrp9thcav@yahoogroups.com) and logged on to the 1/9 webpage (http://cavalier44.my100megs.com). John R "Jack" Schwartz, whose call sign was Cavalier 44, spent a great deal of time and effort in putting the website together He served part of 1970 and '71 in Nam.

What we discovered, as we chatted on the Net, was our memories of the war were very thin, to say the least, and varied greatly. Repeatedly, we shared photos that cracked open the door on suppressed memories. Or someone would mention a situation and the rest brought in their views, which helped to complete an event. We all were searching for long lost buddies, to augment information of actual events, and assist each other with The Ghosts we had all shut into a closet. We often found ourselves discovering names and actions that had been completely erased.

As a rule, e-mails started with someone mentioning a partial memory:
< *E-mail: Anyone remember the time we almost flew into an Arclight?* > And normally responses came, <*Oh yeah, I think it was in late 1970 we were flying on a Pink Team recon near the Cambodian border and all of a sudden the earth came up to meet us.* >

Arclight was the result of B-52s dropping 500lb or 1000lb bombs, which made quite a spectacular fireworks show from miles away, especially at night. Watching the show repeatedly made you thankful the enemy didn't have the same capabilities.

<*Yes, that happened in 71 as well,* > some e-mails responded.>

Our unit was divided into four-color codes. The White team was the fast, agile, and small LOACH (Hughes OH-6 Cayuse Light Observation Helicopters). The Red team consisted of the Cobra Gunship (Bell AH-1G Huey) and our team was the Blue team. In general, the white and red teams flew missions together, which made them the Pink Team; a really menacing color, to be sure.

One such e-mail about an Arclight did bring up some major memories for quite a few of us.

Charlie Troop was assigned to recon the area right after the drop and complete a Bomb Damage Assessment (BDA). Timing was particularly important, because the BDA was to be completed right after the drop to finalize a body count.

Saber Six here, guys, As I recounted on pp 234-244 of "It took Heroes: Volume II, 30 October 1969, I was with the Charlie Troops Blues on standby while a Pink team BDA's a fresh Arclight. I wrote, "We'd been on station a few minutes, circling about...wondering where the pink team was, when suddenly the chopper lurched right into a steep dive to gain speed. I was sitting cross-legged directly behind the left pilot's seat. The violent maneuver caught me off guard. I remained in the aircraft only by catching hold of the doorframe and with the help of troopers deeper inside...Meanwhile, whole trees leaped into the air as a quarter-mile-wide line of explosions marched straight across the area we'd just vacated. It looked as though some trees were coming right at us...We survived the arclight, thanks to the timely arrival and keen eyesight of an Air Force FAC pilot. The FAC had arrived on station after we did and began circling several thousand feet above us...he spotted (us)... the high-flying B-52 bombers had already released their bombs when the FAC warned us to get out of the way...As it was, the last bombs seemed to pass almost beneath us in their angled descent." So I guess this sort of hair-graying experience was not as rare as I thought.— Claude Newby.

One response came like this:

Captain Newby was a Sky Pilot (Chaplain) transferred to Charlie Troop in the prior month. Unlike most Chaplains, Saber Six wanted to be out where he thought he would be needed most, with the troops. He was transferred from a hardcore bush unit because the top brass thought it was too dangerous for him. As the Captain suggested in his book, joining Charlie Troop was hardly any safer.

Most regrettably, my memory erasure was successful. I absolutely forgot the Sky Pilot and the incident on October 30th. I was sitting across from the Chaplain and almost went flying out of the bird as well.

Once the memory was recreated, things opened up about that incident like a gushing oil well. I remembered the dust, dirt, and debris engulfing us all, the taste of the red clay in our mouths, and everyone peppered by sizeable wood splinters. In addition, the mission for the Blues afterwards was to walk the craters for enemy kills and to destroy unexploded bombs.

This operation included destroying one of the 500 pounders. Our resident expert bomb technician Sgt. Richard Dornellas, (the reluctant "Chinese Volunteer" delegated to carry the C-4 explosives) gently approached the ordinance, placed a piece of C-4 on it with a blasting cap and strung about 200 feet of wire.

When Dornellas was set, we found a hole or gully and ducked. We also hoped it would work and we were far enough away. Putting fingers in your ears did not help eliminate the pain from horrendous sound as the massive explosion reverberated through your body.

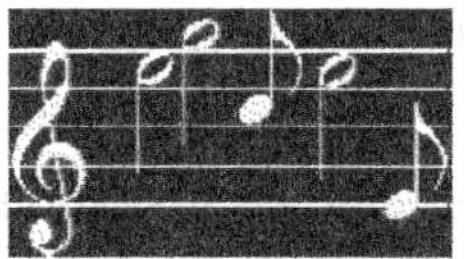

THE MINUTE YOU START TO MESS AROUND

Chapter V - The Ghost of Blue-India

Other recollections of Capt. Newby started to make their way out of the closet. In his book he describes how his first assignment with Charlie Troop was to administer to the funeral of Blue-India who was killed in action September 18, 1969. The funeral was held on Sunday the 21st.

That Sunday I was in Ben Hoa walking down part of a runway with several choppers sitting in revetments. I spotted the yellow circle on the door of a C 1/9 LOACH just across a taxiway and Cavalier White, with some paperwork under his arm, walking toward it. When I approached him, he had this puzzled look on his face.

"*Are you returning to Phouc Vinh,*" I asked.

"*Yes, you're Blue-India, right?*" he responded with a tone of amazement.

"*That's me! Why?...you look surprised.*"

"*Of course I'm surprised!*" he said, "*I attended your funeral this morning.*"

On the flight back to Phouc Vinh, he described how the Blues went out to rescue a LRRP unit in trouble and the word came back that Blue-India was killed in an ambush. The Long Range Recon Patrol, LRRPs as they were called, consisted of five or six guys who sat out in the jungle for days watching enemy movements. More often than not, on the last day of the patrol they would ambush whoever they happened to see. Frequently, the size of the enemy ended up much more than they expected and the Blues were sent in to help out. If the Blues were overwhelmed, they would fly in a hard-core company.

One such LRRP ambush ended with more than 500 NVAs killed after two days of battle. The credit went to the company who came in to get us out, since we were only engaged in the fight for a short period of time.

It was Spec 4 Codis Ray White (Vietnam Wall - Panel: 18W Line 112) who had taken my place for the week I was on Rest and Recuperation (R & R) in Sydney, Australia. Since everyone knew me to be Blue-India it was thought I was the one out with the Blues.

Needless to say, when I signed back into the unit at HQ, the admin clerks had the same shocked reaction. Ray White had only been in the country three months and was the second squad's RTO since early September.

At that point, I had an extremely horrible thought, "*I hope they didn't notify my parents.*" As it turned out, they had the name correct, it was just the rumor mill that was incorrect, as always.

Memories Return

Slowly Memories started to return. The book by Chaplain Newby helped in some ways and shows how in stressful circumstances, such as a firefight, recollections do vary. The memory plays tricks and seems to be very individualized.

The afternoon of the October 30th "Arclight BDA Mission" we were again sent out on another LRRP unit rescue. An ambush was in progress when we arrived in an opening with high elephant grass. The LRRPs were nestled near a tree line 50 feet ahead. When we moved closer we started to take fire from the adjacent woods.

"*Medic...Medic...Medic,*" yelled Blue to our medic in the rear. A bullet hit Spec 4 Roger Eugene Carroll (Panel 16W Line 004) just behind the left ear and below his helmet. He was our 1st squad machine gunner carrying an M60, third in line behind our point and backup. He walked ahead of Blue and me. When he dropped, he fell backward and landed at our feet.

"*Cavalier 22...Cavalier 22, this is Blue-India, come in,*" I yelled into my handset while hitting the dirt. Everyone opened fire with a ferocity that even surprised us.

"*We're taking fire from 270 degrees from our Raspberry Red,*" I continued while popping a red smoke grenade just to the left of the Blues.

"Blue-India, this is Cavalier 22, coming in for a run, best duck!" was the response as the Cobra's blades chattered from the high torque of a fast left turn. Cav 22 was only about 700 feet in the air when he started a barrage of rockets and finished with the miniguns when he was about 150 feet off the ground.

"Cavalier 17 here, coming in for a run," my radio crackled with static as the second Cobra came in seconds after Cav 22 moved out.

AK 47s smacked from all sides telling us we were in the middle of a significant enemy force.

"Cavalier 6, this is Blue-India," was my second call.

"This is Six," our Commanding Officer responded. He was on site to oversee the operation.

"Roger...Six, we need a Medivac. We've got casualties." I reported, hoping the breath I just heard from Carroll was not his last.

"Blue-India, cancel the Medivac," Blue said to me with a stark look and finality which told me we had a KIA.

"Cavalier Six, Cavalier Six, this is Blue-India, cancel our last request, over."

"Blue-India, this is Six, understood," our CO came back with a tone of regret.

Our massive returning fire, and then our Cobra's attack on the enemy's position, repressed the enemy and the firefight subsided. Dusk was setting in and a thunderstorm was swiftly moving our way. We had expended a considerable amount of ammunition and still continued to receive occasional bursts of AK 47s, which was more harassment and aimed at our birds.

Cavalier 6, Major Robert Tredway, flew back to a nearby firebase, loaded his UH-1H with M16 and M60 ammunitions, and returned within ten minutes.

"Blue-India, this is Six, come in."

"This is Blue-India, over," I responded, signaling to Blue that our CO might want to talk to him.

"Roger, got something for you and we can do a pickup," the Major

informed us he had more ammo for us and would be able to pick up Carroll.

"Six, this is Blue-India, we are still taking fire," I was told by Blue to respond and suggest they do a quick flyby and only drop the ammo.

"Understood, will drop what we have, keep your heads down."

When Six arrived he hovered about 30 feet above us, had his crew dump all the ammo, and tried to get out of there without getting shot to pieces. Hovering in midair while taking fire is a gutsy move and makes for an inviting target. The chopper got riddled with AK 47 rounds. I seem to remember Maj. Tredway still managed to hold the chopper still and fly it out of there with a nasty leg wound.

What makes my memory of that day so clear, and why I think it was never put in the closet, it was only one of two nights we spent out in the Jungle. Additionally, the name Roger Carroll never left my mind because there was a morning DJ in Los Angeles with that name. The memory of seeing the head wound was buried and only came back when I read Newby's book.

The difference in what we recollect from that day was Newby remembered all the Blues wearing helmets except for Carroll. I, on the other hand, recall only Carroll wore a helmet.

The imprint of seeing our machine gunner take a bullet just below the helmet gave us a fatalistic view of combat. We all discussed wearing helmets and felt they were too cumbersome, too noisy, and if your time was up…your time was up. The helmet didn't help Carroll. To me, the importance of the memory of the helmet is how time plays tricks and the Chaplain and I have difficulty in recalling exact details.

Newby brought other things to light, which made me laugh as well as scare the hell out of me…once I remembered. In his book, he describes how we spent the night on a trail with thunderstorms continuing most of the night. We just sat down in the high grass and knee-deep mud…filled with repulsive three inch long leaches.

All was quiet except for the normal nighttime jungle sounds…frogs that chirp like birds trying to attract a mate, the occasional flapping of batwings, and howling of a sleepy monkey. Then about 0200 Blue noticed a new sound he did not recognize.

"Did you hear that?" he whispered to Sgt. Gary Ritchason and me.

"Hear what?" I answered, listening more intently thinking he might have heard enemy movement.

"There, I hear it too!" Ritchason said...adding, "Sounds like a growl."

"Maybe it's a tiger," I whispered back, remembering a week earlier a LOACH team had found a Bengal Tiger, killed it, and brought it back as a trophy. The large yellow and black striped male tiger lay for days on the flight line tarmac, empty eyes staring into nothing, huge tongue dangling out, and bullet holes in its majestic fur. It was truly ironic, because of all the horrific things I had seen, one of the saddest was seeing this beautiful creature killed for sport.

"Oh, great," Blue mumbled, "All we need is a tiger looking for a midnight snack of Cordon Blue!"

We tried not to laugh.

"There, I heard it again!" Blue raised up his head to a sound that now seemed to come from several directions.

"Sorry, Blue," I answered, "That's my stomach."

There are things you can control when laying silently in an enemy filled jungle and some things you can't. A guy snoring you can stop; just wake him up and don't let him go to sleep. But once you start laughing and those around you are giggling into their booneyhats, you can't stop it. You try to contain yourself, you know you need to be quiet, but as soon as you stop and the other guy starts laughing again, it's all over.

The Blues had been out in the field since early the prior morning and 18 hours of no food made all our stomachs growl through the rest of the night. We all imagined what the enemy might be thinking, hearing a sound they probably never heard before, wondering if large unknown night creatures were lurking behind some trees or bushes.

In the morning, our Pink Team returned announcing over my radio that a considerable number of crocodiles were surrounding us and as Cavalier 25 said, "Might want to get the hell out of there."

I also regained a memory of the Chaplain, which was not in his book, and I can see why. But I thought it was something that endeared the Captain to all of us as a good shepherd who was down-to-earth and able to relate to the grunts.

"Captain Newby, I'm Blue-India," I told the chaplain as we both boarded the chopper one day. We talked about the confusion of Blue-India being killed and I told him:

"I was on R & R in Australia, Ray White was my replacement."

"Yes, I heard. Good to have you back," he said. *"How was your I & I in Sidney?"*

"I & I???" I asked and said, "Don't you mean R & R?"

"Really, did you Rest and Recuperate? Or was it more like Intoxication and Intercourse?"

"Can't argue that point, chaplain." I responded, thinking this is the coolest chaplain ever.

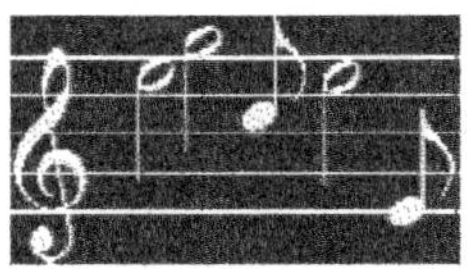

LATE AT NIGHT WHILE YOU'RE SLEEPING

CHARLIE KONG COMES A CREEPIN ALL AROUND

Chapter VI – Another Trooper Down

Lately, more and more messages in our chatroom are heartbreaking and always hit us very hard. As our Webmaster put it so eloquently, "Another trooper has transferred to Fiddler's Green."

The e-mail below, one of many in recent years, announces a Cavalier's Last Charge."

From: Loel Ewart <lewart@>
Subject: Another Cavalier Lost
To: Undisclosed- Recctrp9thcav@yahoogroups.com
Date: Monday, September 8, 2008, 5:24 PM
All

We lost another one.

CW3 (Ret) J.C. Watson of Skipperville, AL lost his battle with Agent Orange last week. He was interned in Ozark. J.C. has been fighting numerous battles and cancers due to Agent Orange and was 100% disabled. He was fairly young at 66. He did a lot of spraying Agent Orange during his tours in RVN.

All that have not had an Agent Orange screening by VA should consider doing so. Loel

February 2002 we received a message announcing Warrant Officer Gary B Hayes (Thirsty 37), a Lift Pilot, succumbed to cancer. In August

David Michael Dzwiglaski, a Helicopter Crewmember, also died after a lengthy bout with cancer. Reality is setting in…Agent Orange is taking its toll!

"Agent Orange (AO) is the code name for an herbicide developed for the military, primarily for use in tropical forests. Although the genesis of the product goes back to the 1940's, serious testing for military applications started in the early 1960's.

The purpose of the product was to deny an enemy cover and concealment in dense terrain by defoliating trees and shrubbery. The product "Agent Orange" (named for the orange band used to mark the drums it was stored in) was principally effective against broad-leaf foliage, such as the dense jungle-like terrain found in Southeast Asia.

The product was tested in Vietnam in the early 1960's, and brought into ever widening use during the height of the war (1967-69). Its use was diminished and eventually discontinued in 1971.

Agent Orange was a 50-50 mix of two chemicals, known conventionally as 2,4,D and 2,4,5,T. The combined product was mixed with kerosene or diesel fuel and dispersed by aircraft, vehicle, and hand spraying. An estimated 19 million gallons of Agent Orange were used in South Vietnam during the war.

The earliest health concerns about Agent Orange were about the product's contamination with TCDD, or dioxin. TCDD is one of a family of dioxins, some found in nature, and are cousins of the dibenzofurans and pcb's.

The TCDD found in Agent Orange is thought to be harmful to man. In laboratory tests on animals, TCDD has caused a wide variety of diseases, many of them fatal. TCDD is not found in nature, but rather is a man-made and always unwanted byproduct of the chemical manufacturing process. The Agent Orange used in Vietnam was later found to be extremely contaminated with TCDD."
(http://www.lewispublishing.com/range.htm,May 2008)

The triple canopy Vietnamese jungle made fighting the enemy extremely difficult. You were in a world of darkness unable to see more than a couple of feet ahead. Every bush or tree made a good hiding place for a high casualty ambush.

We could see the use of Agent Orange was making an impact on the jungle. By 1969, AO had significantly reduced the foliage to a point where you could see well for 30 to 50 feet. For us, it was an advantage that reduced the chances of an inescapable firefight. We could see the enemy and that was fine with us. The cost of whatever AO was going to inflict in the future was worth being able to go home and live another 30 or so years.

Ground units walking around in the stuff, understandably, were at a high risk of absorbing the toxins. Yet, it now is apparent those in Helicopter Attack units, with choppers blowing up so much dust and debris, were even at higher risk.

Congress in the 1980's finally asked the Veterans Administration to investigate the possibility of AO causing health problems for the 2.5 million who served in Vietnam. Due to inaction by both Congress and the VA, an "Agent Orange" product liability, class action lawsuit was filed involving more than 200,000 veterans. The suit was against seven chemical manufacturing companies for injuries the veterans and family members believed were caused by AO and other herbicides used in Nam. A settlement of $180 million was reached in 1984.

Since then the VA has increased its research concerning the healthcare effects and now recognizes the following conditions as service-connected:

Chloracne – a skin disorder

Porphyria Cutanea Tarda – a skin disorder

Acute or Subacute Transient Peripheral Neuropathy –a nerve disorder. Peripheral neuropathy is a nervous system condition that causes numbness, tingling, and muscle weakness by involvement of the nerves, that is, neural conducting tissue outside the brain and spinal cord (http://www.geocities.com/pentagon/bunker/8212/briefD5.html)

Type 2 Diabetes – In type 2 diabetes, either the body does not produce enough insulin or the cells ignore the insulin. Insulin is necessary for the body to be able to use glucose for energy.

Cancer–

Non-Hodgkin's Lymphoma – a cancer that starts in the lymphoid tissue. Such tissue makes up the lymph nodes, spleen, and other organs of the immune system.

Chronic Lymphocytes Leukemia – (also known as "chronic lymphoid leukemia" or "CLL"), is a type of leukemia, Hodgkin's Disease – Hodgkin's lymphoma is characterized clinically by the orderly spread of disease from one lymph node group to another.

Multiple Myeloma – a type of cancer of plasma cells which are immune system cells in bone marrow that produces antibodies. Myeloma is regarded as incurable.

Prostate Cancer – a disease in which cancer develops in the prostate, a gland in the male reproductive system.

Respiratory Cancers - (including cancers of the lung, larynx, trachea, and bronchus.

Chronic Lymphocytic Leukemia – a particular lymphocyte, the B cell, which originates in the bone marrow, develops in the lymph nodes, and normally fights infection.

(Wikipedia Free Dictionary: http://en.wikipedia.org/wiki/Hodgkin's_disease)

I remember receiving an e-mail on August 18, 2002, notifying us that Dzwiglaski had passed away. It was a Sunday morning when I was about to e-mail my daughter to wish her happy birthday. Instead I sat down and wrote the following for Daviski (his nickname) and offered it to his family as a memorial to a past comrade in arms.

A Cavalier's Last Charge

A Cavalry Soldier passed on the Stetson and Sword today.
Boots at rest...taps echoed once again.
Flagpoles stand at half; the banner flies stoutly with the wind.

A Cavalry Soldier stepped off a "Winged Horse" today.
Troopers stand with heels pressed taut...adorned with glazed eyes.
Flattened hands pushed temple tight, for one's last combat flight.

A Cavalry Soldier died today, with honor forged on infinity's wall.
Long vanished Cavaliers proudly join the final charge,
So Remembrance could speak the name... for eternity's present roll-call.

Most Vietnam Vets who slowly transfer to Fiddler's Green don't complain or want anything special, while nearly all deem it is part of the service to this country. What I discovered, while communicating with these heroes, is that very few feel they did anything out of the ordinary.

Many of our pilots jeopardized everything to get us out of trouble. Moreover, they knew the Blues would go to any lengths to recover those involved in a downed bird. It was just part of what needed to be done. Today, the fight with Agent Orange and PTSD is also part of that.

For the most part, the VA Health System is working well with Vets and now those who seek medical attention for Agent Orange related problems have a much easier road than those who had a long and difficult struggle in the mid to late 1980's and early 1990's. Hopefully, Vietnam paved the way for better care for all of our heroes of today and better care has been one of the many positive results from the War in Vietnam.

VI..ET..N..AM...VI..ET..N..AM

Chapter VI I –Brothers Pushed Into the Closet

One quandary with pushing your bad memories into an inaccessible closet is you also put things in it which should not be there. Anything related to Nam is quickly dumped behind the door without regard to what it is.

The names of those...who returned home in flag covered coffins... should be branded in your memory never to be forgotten. Or, for that matter, those who you served with should also always be honored.

For me, six names fit into that category: Spec 4 Codis Ray White (KIA), Spec 4 Roger Eugene Carroll (KIA), Staff Sgt. Richard Dornellas, 1st Lt. Glenn A (Buddha) Jenkins, Sgt. Freeman (Duffy) Daugherty, and Staff Sgt. Gary Ritchason. Of course there should be many more. However, these are larger than life heroes and are part of the memories I put in with the "Ghost in the Orange Closet."

Contact with Blue-Mike

I mailed a "get reacquainted" letter in early 2001 to Gary Ritchason who lived in the Chicago area. He was listed in the phonebook and two days later I received a surprise phone call.

"Hi, Tom, this is Sergeant Gary Ritchason, old Blue-Mike," a familiar and friendly voice said. Even after so many years, I still recognized his voice, which I really found interesting. So much buried in the closet...but not the voice of an old friend.

"Gary? Wow, it's good to hear from you," I said, shocked at the call since the letter was just mailed.

"Yeah, the last contact I had with you was a card from Palm Springs, showing you made it home." Gary reminded me. He made it home a couple of months before I did.

"Yes, I still remember putting guard towers on the desert postcard," I said, remembering for the first time I had written him when I got home.

Gary Ritchason was Blue-Mike, the platoon sergeant from May 1969 to February 1970. He was genuinely what one would imagine a platoon sergeant to be; strong, stocky, athletic, squared chin, and a formidable man. In other words, he could be the Poster Sergeant for the Army. As Blue-Mike, he exuded confidence and outstanding leadership and a sense of humor that made him fun to be around.

No doubt he excelled in baseball and football in high school and when we managed to get a volleyball game together, he was usually the top player. He was a bright guy just married before he left for Nam. You could tell he was devoted to his wife Dee, whom he was still married to when we spoke.

The phone call reminded me of his athletic ability and that it wasn't just useful in sports. In late June 1969, the Blues went out to recon a very fresh contact area. Early in the afternoon several of our choppers got riddled with bullets when they surveyed an area with fresh trails. Their call to us suggested a large group of hostiles was moving through the area and we should investigate.

We had already been inserted twice that day with no contact and thought we were heading home. The call came, "One more stop." Superstition always made us leery about the "one more" bit. The LZ (Landing Zone) was safe enough and we moved west on a trail our scout birds found. Just as we moved about 100 meters north into the jungle, we came under heavy fire.

"Pop a Raspberry, Blue-Mike," Blue instructed Gary. We used "Banana" yellow smoke to signal our location and a "Raspberry" Red smoke for the enemy. Since he had the best arm, he tossed the red smoke right in the middle of the suspected hostiles.

"Blue-India, get some fire on that smoke," Blue instructed me to get our Cobra Gunship to unload some of its ammo on the red smoke. The venom of the cobra's attack made us all duck for deeper cover.

"Grenade! Grenade!" was the call, as one of those strange

Russian hand grenades bounced in the middle of the Blues. Blue-Mike jumped up and like a second basemen completing a double play, swooped up the grenade, tossed it back at the enemy, and hit the dirt. It exploded just over the enemy.

The firefight lasted another few seconds with the Blues doing all the firing and the NVA's scurrying back into the thick jungle. Between the cover bird's rockets and miniguns, and our firepower; the NVA decided not to stay around.

I doubt anyone who had not played baseball would have been able to make the move Gary made with no seconds to spare. His regard for his men and quick action saved quite a few, including Blue and me. He was awarded the coveted Bronze Star with a V for Valor for that action.

Our phone conversation that day went quite well. I was in the midst of cancer treatment, which I explained. He was within a couple of years from retiring from a utility company, has two grown daughters, and all seemed to be quite good. He had his good sense of humor.

"So, you still fall down a lot?" Gary asked. Carrying a 25 lb radio and 30 lbs of ammo, about 30% of my body weight, made me top heavy and prone to landing head first. I never gave it a second thought and even felt it might be an advantage if we walked into an ambush.

"No, not since I gave up carrying the radio. Now I just fall down when I've had a few too many," I told him.

He did ask what the names were of the two KIAs the Blues had in '69. Terrible as it may sound, we both botched their names and only later found out exactly who they were.

That was it! I was planning a trip to Chicago about six months later and wanted to see if he wanted to meet and have a few beers. I never heard from him again. We received Christmas cards, signed by Dee, no contact by e -mail or returned calls.

I was really disappointed. I liked Gary. We spent numerous after hours together and struck up what I thought was a good friendship. Not hearing again made me think I said something to upset him. After several attempts, I did mention my contact with Gary to Walker Jones. He acknowledged he had the same experiences with several brothers he contacted.

"They would be excited about the contact and said they would pull out the photo album," Jones stated, *"But they never called back!"* He also thought he had said something, but later realized it was a common occurrence experienced by many who looked to re-establish contacts but could not face The Ghost.

It made me feel better. Yet, I had hoped to sit down with Ritchason and see what he remembered and how his struggles with those memories were going. He was, at times, a quiet person who kept things inside...usually a sign The Ghost was nailed in the closet, never to see the light of day again.

One additional factor really made sense and I'm sure many Vets who buried Ghosts were seriously affected by the attack on the World Trade Center on September 11, 2001. VA doctors advised me such a catastrophic event has catapulted many into Post Traumatic Stress Disorder.

Searching for Duffy

The first Vietnam assignment Freeman "Duffy" Daugherty and I were given was two weeks of KP in an officers' mess in Saigon. Duffy and I had been together since basic training at Fort Ord, California, and managed to stay together through Advanced Infantry Training (AIT) and special weapons training at Hunter Ligget, CA. He and I would hang together when off base. Naturally, as young testosterone filled guys, the only thing on our minds was meeting some nice local girls and discuss the weather.

Duffy was a surfer from Oceanside, CA. with blonde hair and a kind of surfer "Hang Loose" demeanor. He was about six feet tall, with broad shoulders, a big Hollywood smile, and a look which attracted the ladies. Hanging around him was always an adventure filled with a knack for finding parties or creating some at the spur of the moment.

We both received orders to leave for Nam on the same flight from Oakland to Saigon with layovers in Seattle and Tokyo. The Major, who was in charge of the flight, was apparently extremely offended when we accidentally delayed the take-off in Seattle. Duffy and I had met two

Stewardesses, as they were called then, during the three-hour layover. We walked with them to the far end of the airport to find some quiet place to discuss world affairs.

"That looks like your plane on the taxiway," one of the young ladies observed.

"Holy Shit, that is our plane," we said in agreement. A quick kiss goodbye and a promise to write, and we raced back to our gate. The plane was at the end of the taxiway ready for takeoff before they got the word we were not aboard. It seemed like it took the plane forever to turn around and come back. We both felt we were in deep manure if the plane took off.

Truthfully, the only thing saving us from being considered AWOL and in real trouble was the airport was under substantial renovation and the intercom system only worked in parts of the airport. Also, two Marines missed the last call for our flight, so our excuse was reluctantly accepted.

We chuckled when the Major gave us a stern warning for being irresponsible and delaying the flight. *"What are they going to do, not send us to Nam?"* Duffy asked me. When we heard KP duty for two weeks…we smiled thinking it beat being in the jungle.

The two weeks on KP went too fast. The duty was really not bad, except for having to get up at 0400 each morning. It started with peeling numerous potatoes, cleaning up the mess the cook was making, and doing dishes. Things changed for the better for both of us on the third day. Duffy had experience slinging hash at a hamburger joint, which the cook quickly recognized and put him to work in the kitchen.

My experience was working for a bakery in Germany before school each morning when I was eleven. Old Herr Kuhn would have been proud to know his training would serve the Officers mess in Saigon one day. I was lucky. Once the bread was made and the rolls out of the oven cooling off, my shift was done.

Duffy needed to prep for lunch, but he was also finished working by eleven. Besides, by that time we were higher than a kite.

"Man I feel bitchin'," Duffy yelled over to me during one of the first few days in the mess, while throwing some lettuce my way.

"I know what you mean, this stuff is a gas," as I returned fire with a hot bun, which he caught and munched on. For some reason we really got the munchies about that time, looking for anything sweet we could find.

Duffy took me to the side one day and said, "*You know what that shit is, don't you?*"

"*What...what is?*" I said

"*The shit those guys are smoking over there!*"

"*Yeah, they're smoking pipes, so what?*" I said in a rather naïve tone.

"*No, man, they're smoking dope,*" he laughed, as we both looked at the Vietnamese pot scrubbers who worked in the kitchen. They took breaks every half hour and smoked Hashish. Duffy and I got high just from the fumes.

With a great buzz going, we spent the rest of the day in the NCO Club drinking beer, hypnotized by the fan blades. I can still hear the music from the Chamber Brothers and their hit, "Time Has Come." KP definitely beat slashing away with a machete in the jungle.

When we received our new orders, we reluctantly left the KP behind and were sent north to An Khe to the 1st Cav headquarters which actually was in the midst of a move down to Ben Hoa. We both hoped we would end up in the same unit, but unfortunately, Duffy got the worst deal. He was assigned to A Troop 1st of the 12th Cavalry who stayed out in the jungle for months.

He and I communicated through a few letters and postcards and once met while on the same highway before we went into combined action against a sizeable force of NVA's.

Duffy served with great honor. He was wounded three times and awarded two Bronze Stars with V devices. When we did talk about his experience, he mentioned he was wounded twice in the shoulder and once in the leg. The two shoulder wounds came from friendly chopper fire while in the midst of being overrun at firebase Dolly.

"*I don't know who invented the word friendly-fire, but the pain is the same friendly or not,*" I remember him telling me.

In the end, we actually came home on the same flight. This time we didn't delay the flight in Seattle.

Still Searching

In 2004, I looked for Duffy in the Southern California area and called several numbers of an F. Daugherty, but with no success. I sent one letter to a Duffy Daugherty in Escondido, CA. and I received a very nice phone call from a young woman who said her husband goes by Duffy but he never served in the military. She did indicate they had heard there was another Duffy in Carlsbad. I sent letters to the last name of Daugherty in the Southern California area hoping to get a response, but none came.

Recently, I sent out eleven letters again to all the addresses in Southern California listed under Daugherty and all but three came back with "return to sender – attempted –not known." I still occasionally look for phone numbers to call to see if I can reach my old friend, but nothing so far.

Nevertheless, like so many others, he may have buried his Ghost too deep and does not want to open the door fearing what monster might come out. Many of the Charlie Troopers who went searching for brothers found the same scenario. Even when you did find and contacted a friend, they responded with great enthusiasm during the call, but found it too difficult to pull more out of the closet. Often we never heard from them again.

Dornellas: What a Character

Staff Sgt. Richard Dornellas came to the Blues in the latter part of May 1969. When he showed up, he was in the second half of his second tour. He walked into the NCO hut with tailored Tiger Stripped South Vietnamese camouflage fatigues, a German Infantry Cap, and an Iron Cross around his neck. He was 5 ft. 6 inches tall and weighed about 140 lbs, just a hair taller than most of the Vietnamese we were fighting. Of Italian descent, Dornellas' records showed he hailed from Pensacola, Florida, but he grew up in New York and considered himself a New Yorker.

His first tour he was with an armored unit which he claimed, "Didn't have enough action," so he volunteered to join the 1st of the 9th as a door gunner for his second tour. Needless to say, he found war exciting and wanted to see more action. After seeing the Blues going out into the field on a daily basis, he requested a transfer to join us.

Richard Dornellas was a soldier first and a prankster second. When not out in the jungle with the Blues, he was always looking for ways to create some excitement. If it was going to create some laughs he was willing to instigate it. It wasn't unlike him to take a grenade apart, remove the blasting cap, and put it back together. At an appropriate moment, he would pull the pin and toss the frag in the middle of some partiers, just to see them scramble. Then he would calmly walk over and pick it up, stating, "It's only a dud!"

Just because he came flying into our hootch seconds before a frag blew up one of our neighbor's latrines, did not necessarily mean he was the one who did it. That's what Blue-Mike told the rather irate LRRP Captain whose shitter was in shambles and a rather large quantity of its contents over his uniform.

It was really never established who blew up the latrine, but those of us who bunked with Dornellas knew the smile on his face, when the subject came up, was one of utter satisfaction.

Richard volunteered for the most dangerous missions, usually arclight bomb disposals, and was always the first on the flight line when the "Downed Bird" call came across the camp. He actually enjoyed walking point or rearguard. To him, war was exciting, a great rush, and he was fixated by it. That's not to say he wasn't affected by those who died, he just wanted to do the best he could to prevent people in his platoon from getting hurt. We all felt if there was anyone who would throw himself on a grenade to save others, he would be the one.

The day Carroll died and had to be carried to another landing zone, Richard was the first to take his shirt off to make a stretcher. Blue-Mike was the other. Our trek was cut short due to nightfall and thunderstorms, so we just stopped, went horizontal, and tried to survive the night. The fact we all were in a foot of swamp didn't make any difference. However, it made a difference to Dornellas.

"That's it!" he told us the next day. *"I'm not washing these pants until I leave Nam."* He had decided his fatigues were lucky and you don't mess with that kind of lucky charm. He promised never to have them cleaned again, at least until he was stateside. From that day on the sergeant always

stopped to change into his lucky pants before going out on any missions. He became a real quick-change artist on "Downed Bird" calls. Calling the pants lucky was his way of controlling his own destiny.

"That's fine," I told him, and added, *"Just keep the smell away from me."* He had the bunk next to mine and I could just imagine what those pants would smell like in two more months.

The Fortuneteller

Richard was a favorite with the hootch maids. He spoke a little Vietnamese and made an effort putting them to work in his little corner, which he rewarded with some cash. He also managed to get one of the maids, who professed to be skilled in reading Tarot cards, to tell us our future. She was an older woman who spoke English with a combination French and Vietnamese accent. She apparently was schooled in a French school in Saigon where they also taught English. Her fortune telling skills supposedly came from her grandmother who lived in the village just outside our base camp.

"Come on, bring your cards," the second tour soldier teased the woman and then said something in Vietnamese.

"No, you come village, I read card there," she always responded, probably thinking it wasn't a good idea to read someone's fortune outside the village.

"Bring the cards and everyone will pay you beaucoup d'argent," was his response while gesturing his fingers to show money was involved.

"No, no, not good for soldier see cards, no good, beaucoup mal, C'est non bonne chance," she said, which meant it was bad luck. But little did she know the persuasive powers of this sergeant, or it might have just been she got tired of being hassled about it. She did bring the cards one day while Dornellas, Sgt Cornilias Winship, and I were waiting for chowtime.

She sat on Winship's bunk and used his footlocker as a table and began to shuffle her cards. Winship, who was a rather mild and good-natured full-blooded Indian, decided he would be first and sat down beside her.

"I don't believe in this shit, but what the heck," he said, with a kind

of nervous smile. He gave her a five-dollar multicolored script note that was used for money over there. The Greenback was not circulated in the war zone.

She masterfully swept up the money, drew two cards, and placed them facedown on the locker, then drew three more cards and placed them face-up below the initial two. She then placed one card face-up above all the cards.

"You be successful in life," she said, which raised a smile from Winship, and then with his typical cynicism, profoundly stated, *"Keep this up and I might start believing."*

The hootchmaid drew another card and placed it face-up on the locker and looked at her five-dollar patron with a smile.

"There be many strong woman in your life," paused a few seconds, turned over another card and then finished her sentence, "Which will cause you lutte' and beaucoup tristesse."

"What does that mean?"

"Beaucoup strife and sadness," she explained.

"Leave my mother out of this," he retorted, laughed, and looked around to see if we were laughing as well. We were!

She then, with a rather serious tone in her eyes, preceded to carefully turnover the two facedown cards. She said, *"You go home with pain, but it go away."*

We didn't know what to make of the last part except he might be wounded yet go home safe and sound. Winship never brought it up and neither did we.

It was difficult for me to interpret the reading and whether I should take it seriously. I had my doubts, but yet it was well known in Germany, where I grew up, that Gypsies possessed the power of foretelling events. We had several Gypsies who lived in our town who were admired for their abilities and many thought their gift was something to respect. In other words, I was very hesitant to hear what she might tell me about my future. She did make a convincing presentation and her body language suggested she was very much in earnest about the comments she made.

Sometimes it's best not to know too much about what might happen. There is the thought of a self-fulfilling prophecy. Regardless, I sat down on the floor opposite the mystic and placed a ten-dollar note on the locker and watched it disappear. I had expected to have some change come back, but that was not her idea. My resolution was maybe the additional five would enhance my chances of getting a better reading from her cards.

She proceeded to lay the cards out in a different fashion. First she put down three, all facedown. Then she placed four face-up and then again a single card on top. My apprehension grew to the point where my pulse rate was higher than when I looked out of our choppers' open doors at two-thousand feet.

"Your family didn't come from Gypsies, did they?" I asked, half expecting her to have French ties to those wanderers of Europe.

"Ggeepsies, what is Ggeepsiiis?" she asked me with this look that either meant she was fully aware of what Gypsies were and their reputation, or she was being coy about her ignorance.

"Never mind!" I said quickly, *"Just give me the good news. I don't want to hear the bad."*

"I read cards, bien ou mal. OK?"

I knew that would be her response and settled for the fact if it was good news I would believe her and if "mal," I would just dismiss it as BS. She smiled when she turned over the first card.

"You will have two Babysons," she said with a wistful smile and added, *"Also deux femme'... madams."*

"Two wives?" I questioned.

"Yes, two!" she stated rather convincingly.

"I will have two wives... at the same time?" I said jokingly

"Non, non, not same time," she laughed openly as did the others.

"You make beaucoup money and get old, bien de vie," she smiled a soft incisive smile that I can still picture today. I was satisfied my extra five was getting me much better results than I expected. But then I thought, *"Two wives maybe beaucoup mal."*

The tone of the session was actually now quickly taking the

unbelievers into a more serious questioning mode. Is she for real?

Dornellas was next and he sat down beside her, put his arm around her shoulders and told her to proceed. She placed the cards down on the locker in the same manner she had used for my reading. She had a displeasing look on her face from the moment she turn up the first face card. You could see in her face she liked this American and thought him to be "Le Drole American," funny American who made jokes about everything.

The hootchmaid turned several cards over and said nothing. Then, she quickly turned the three down cards over and almost in the same motion collected them all and started to get up. The sergeant's arm on her shoulder kept her from moving too far.

"What's up?" he asked, with a frown on his face like he was being cheated out of his five bucks.

"You will not go home, so sorry, you made me...you made me do this," she turned her face from Dornellas and cried. Then she pushed up again, made her way around the footlocker and dashed out the screen door.

Obviously, we questioned her readings and made excuses. *"She's full of shit!"* we all said in hopes of appeasing a concerned fellow soldier. And we all tried to put a positive slant on it.

"Sure, that means you're going to stay here, marry a Vietnamese and have beaucoup Babysons," we all told him.

"That's fine, I like the weather here and I feel tall," he answered with a smirk.

"Saddle up, we've got a mission," was announced by Ritchason running through our hootch, just in time.

"Let's go have some fun," responded our prankish sergeant in hopes of lifting our spirits and forgetting what just transpired. He claimed he hated to sit around, but it was obvious he enjoyed the rush danger presented and we all knew he wanted to prove the fortune teller was wrong.

"It's a downed Cobra, the crew is safe. We just need to help retrieve the bird," we were told when we hopped on our transport. The Cobra had mechanical problems; managed to auto-rotate down to a nice LZ and the pink team partner pulled the crew to safety. Now, several choppers were prowling

the area to make certain the enemy would stay away from this expensive piece of equipment. It was still fully loaded with 14 rockets, 4,000 rounds of 7.62 mm "minigun" ammo, and 250 grenades from its 40 mm grenade launcher.

This mission found us with what we considered a full complement of 19 Blues. We were informed the LZ was cold and in a nice open area not too far from Phouc Vinh. They were right; the flight only took us a couple of minutes. By the time we got on station to secure the area and prepare the bird to be hauled back to the base, a Hook (Boeing CH-47 Chinook Transport Helicopter) arrived creating strong swirling winds and tiny dust fragments hit our faces as it maneuvered over its target

We received instructions on how to hook the Cobra to the 50-foot tether line. Naturally, our favorite volunteer sergeant was happy to step forward and attempt the acrobatics needed to hook the two birds together. He had experience hooking tanks together, so this should be a piece of cake. Climbing on top of the gunship's rotors was a cinch for the agile New Yorker, but with the wind circling from the Hook, catching the tether was another story. The line swung in counter-clock-wise motion just inches out of his reach.

"Give me my 16," he shouted down with exasperation after about six attempts to catch the towline. We weren't sure if he was going to use it to increase his reach or to take some pot shots at the Hook's crew. Not only was the wind from the Hook causing problems, so was the 20 mph wind from the weather front with heavy rains heading our way.

The M-16 was a good idea. The connection was completed and our fellow Blue scrambled down from his high perch, but not before giving us some comedic poses. His antics made everyone laugh and we relaxed knowing this job was almost complete and we should be back in our nice dry hootches before the raindrops fell.

"Hooker 4-7, this is Blue-India, you're a go! Over," I called to the transport to let him know our man was clear and they could proceed.

"Roger, Blue-India, we have a positive GO! Thanks for the hookup. Hooker 4-7, out!"

I squelched my handset twice as a courtesy response as the tether tightened. Dornellas was all smiles, picked up his gear, and joined Blue and I a few feet from the Cobra that was starting to lift off the ground. The Hook leisurely climbed vertically for about 30 feet, showing the strain from the more than 10,000 lbs in tow. It was a great sight to watch the bird's slow climb. The gunship started a natural circular rotation as the wind pushed it to a streamline position.

Then, the tether snapped! The Hook catapulted skyward, leaving the Cobra in mid air. Time stopped long enough for the three of us to shout, "Oh, shit!" Blue pushed me into a ditch; then jumped in right beside me. Dornellas scrambled behind a large termite mount and the rest of the Blues, knowing a massive explosion of fuel and armaments was to follow, hit the dirt where they stood.

Fourteen rockets launched sporadically, two or three at a time, exploding in the nearby tree line. The M-40 grenades popped like popcorn at a movie theater, just with piercing detonations. The heat was immense and the only salvation, for those of us who weren't smart enough to stand far way, was that we were several feet below the elevation of the explosions and fire.

The 250 grenades took a good 30 minutes to burst, sending shrapnel and flames all over the LZ. Even covering our ears did little to deaden the earth-shattering blasts. After about an hour, the intensity of the flames finally started to set off the 7.62 mm rounds. At times just one or two cracked past our heads and other times 20 or 30 rounds ripped into the air, trees, and ground.

The entire show was now past the two-hour mark. Our cover birds had scrambled out of the area to avoid the not-so-friendly fire. With the choppers' fuel getting low, they returned to Phouc Vinh, leaving the Blues alone to fend for themselves in a one directional firefight.

The last few rounds of the 4,000 the bird had in its belly went off just as the first drops of rain hit us. Almost as abrupt as the crash of the Cobra came on us, so did the heavy tropical storm. The fire was being doused, which was encouraging, but the water was also getting quite high in the ditches we temporarily called home. As most tropical storms, this one lasted about a half an hour. Our transport choppers came and lifted the Blues from the now parched and soaked LZ. The Blues were lucky again. No one injured, no one hurt, just pissed off and wet to the core.

We hit the showers when we got back, clothes and all. All, that is, except our friend Dornellas. Four months of his lucky and extremely dirty pants was beginning to have an affect on all his hootch mates, especially those near his bunk. The smell was getting to the point where we asked him to hang the pants outside.

He refused, we put up with the smell since we didn't want to jinx his lucky charm. Additionally, we all wanted to see if his prediction of the pants eventually "standing on their own" would come true.

Sure enough, early one December afternoon in 1969, we came back from another muddy and wet mission when Dornellas took his pants off and actually stood them up in the middle of the floor.

"Hey guys, look at this!" he shouted, as we gathered around in disbelief. They looked like papier-mâché pants, fully rounded and like in a cartoon where inanimate objects take on a life of their own. These pants could easily walk away. Dornellas was as proud as a father with a newborn babe. The rest of the Blues and some pilots came by to witness the event. We laughed, opened a case of beer, and celebrated him going home, which he did.

With great relief, we denounced the fortuneteller's prediction that he would never make it home; even though her prediction on Sgt. Winship had come true. In late November in a firefight he was shot in the left elbow and went home with that wound. When we received a letter and picture showing Dornellas in the Florida sunshine at Christmas time, we were relieved.

Then...news came in the last days of January 1970...Staff Sgt. Richard Dornellas died in a tank at the beginning of his third tour. The news hit us all quite hard. We liked the guy and were saddened to see the fortuneteller was right after all. (Staff Sgt. Richard Dornellas - KIA 1/27/70 Panel 14, Line 71)

Still Searching for Buddha Jenkins

On one reminiscing occasion my e-mail to the chatroom was, *<anyone remember Lt. Glenn A Jenkins, Cavalier Blue 69? >*

John Powell, Cavalier 24, e-mailed back: *< "Buddha Jenkins," remember him well, have pictures and lots of stories, would like to hear yours!">*

He also inquired whether anyone had been able to contact him. I had totally forgotten about the "Buddha" nickname. Once I read the name, numerous memories starting pouring into my head. Many were good ones of missions we had successfully completed, nights we shared too many beers, tons of laughs, scotch, chick stories, and the memories of hot firefights.

Lt. Glenn A. Jenkins came to the Blues in May 1969 and his introduction was during a rocket attack that strangely enough happened in an early afternoon. After the January, 1969 Tet Offensive by the NVA, our base camp, Phouc Vinh, was constantly rocketed at 0100 and 0300 hours. The norm was one or two rockets, but sometimes quite a few more.

The night before our introduction to the new Cavalier Blue, there was nothing. Our thought was maybe we finally got the guys responsible. We knew they were local, but just never could catch them.

Our night patrols scurried around the sites we thought the rockets were being launched, but those Viet Cong were no dummies. Fortunately, they also were very inaccurate and rarely did more than just make potholes. However, after the daytime attack, the rockets came day or night…and with greater accuracy.

One day Jenkins was walking to our hut when he spotted a Vietnamese worker who looked like he was repairing the roof of a large helicopter repair hanger. When he looked again he noticed the worker writing down things on a piece of paper.

At that point, we certainly didn't know our new platoon leader or the kind of humor and demeanor he had. He was a husky guy with a round face, scruffy mustache, and broad smile. He showed up at our first platoon meeting with a North Vietnamese helmet, holstered pistol with a white pearl handle, cigarette in his mouth, and a radio on his back. When he walked in the hut, he put the radio down and said, *"Who's Blue-Mike?"*

"*I am, Lieutenant,*" a voice came from the group.

"*Here, find someone to carry this,*" he said, handing over the radio.

"*Roger, Blue*!" was the somewhat surprised response. The prior Blue carried his own radio and had Blue-India work in the second squad. It was a quick promotion and in many ways it showed how Jenkins looked at us as professionals and trusted us to do the jobs assigned. He delegated well and the men respected that.

He also had a very dry sense of humor that took some getting used to. "*Was he joking?*" came to be a saying we latched on to until we understood the things he thought were funny. That's why we had such a great laugh when he came into our hooch with a big grin.

"*Three Blues come with me, with 16s locked and loaded! Safety on.*"

"*Right Blue,*" several of us responded and followed him across the road to one of the larger hangers. He was looking around like he was searching for something particular, still smiling, or more like laughing to himself.

"*You're probably wondering why I brought you here.*" Blue said, as we came to the side of the hanger. We thought it might be a joke, but why did we have to bring loaded weapons?

"*Well, look around. See anything strange?*" he asked.

We looked up and down the road, back the way we came, and around the building, but no…nothing looked strange.

"*Look up on this hanger, guys.*"

"*Hey, there is a guy stuck up there on the roof,*" we all said, getting ready to grab the ladder lying on the ground.

"*Don't you guys find this strange? There is a worker on this roof with no tools!*"

The presumed worker was stranded 20 plus feet in the air because Jenkins had taken down the ladder. When we forced the rather reluctant Vietnamese off the roof and searched him, we uncovered several small-sketched maps of the compound. Now we knew why they had become more accurate in their rocket attacks.

During the first few weeks with our new leader we never saw him without his helmet on. When we observed him without it, it was a complete shock. He was bald! The head was completely shaved, which in those days was rare, especially in the military. It was also no surprise Blue became known as Buddha Jenkins to his fellow officers.

Blue acclimated to life on the ground rather quickly. Lt. Jenkins relished the leadership assignment and made the best of it. Following several weeks of recon missions and a couple of "Downed Birds," Blue made significant changes in how we operated. First we stripped down to the minimum. No sleeping bags, food, gas masks, or flack jackets. He asked us to load up with ammo, water, and go light.

"*Bring a candy bar if you think you're going to get hungry*," he told us.

His thought was to move silently. In the past we rarely walked the trails used by the enemy; expecting them to be booby-trapped. Now, Blue's analysis was we were in the jungle with the North Vietnamese who in fact didn't know the area any better than we did. Booby-traps would be dangerous for them as well as us. The tactic was clever because moving with such a stealth approach enabled us to repeatedly surprise and ambush the enemy.

Jenkins also was very thorough in how we entered a hot Landing Zone (LZ) and how we exited the Hueys. He was the first one off and last one on the birds. The RTO followed, and our machine gunners next. Firepower and communications were his priority and to his credit it worked extremely well. We only lost two people during his leadership because of his changes and concern for his men. He also was adamant about how we approached "Downed Birds." Blue-Mike, Blue-India, and one machine gunner were on 24/7 emergency standby.

The start of the Monsoons also changed at what time we went out on missions. Most of our missions started early in the morning so we could be back at the base camp by late afternoons when the daily deluge arrived. Neither he nor the rest of the Blues relished the thought of spending nights out in the jungle, not when we had nice comfortable cots and a fridge full of beer waiting.

I especially remember one endless day in June of 1969, which started with an uneventful reconnaissance mission. We scurried around the jungle for several hours and found nothing. Our transports picked us up and dropped us in another area where we searched for hours with no results. Then, as the afternoon monsoon clouds swiftly moved in from the east and night was looming, we hustled onto our choppers and went back to Phouc Vinh.

Most of us had showered, finally dried out, and were comfortable as the night settled in.

"*Saddle up, we have a Downed Bird,*" Blue-Mike shouted as he made his way through our four hootches. We jumped, grabbed our gear, and within minutes were airborne.

I can still see how the darkness beneath us was like an endless black sea with waves that seemingly reach up and down several hundred feet. Valleys covered with elephant grass and natural breaks in the terrain had a deeper shade of blackness than the jungle tree lines. Directly ahead, the scattered cumulous clouds partially shadowed the waxing crescent moon. You could still smell the freshness of that evening's Monsoon rain...and the underlying, ever present, smell of gunpowder and military equipment.

Three UH-1E helicopters were flying a thousand feet above the jungle terrain. The engines howled and rotors flapped with the same sense of urgency the pilots were pushing the envelope of their choppers' top speed. One of our choppers was down, the crew was in danger, and it was our job to get to them.

"Downed Birds" was a rescue mission, which had to be carried out with precision and daring courage by the pilots. Our job was to get there, rescue the crew, bring them to safety and, of course, to make sure the expensive piece of military hardware did not fall into enemy hands.

"*Did you see how many made the other choppers?*" Blue asked me, one hand cupped around his mouth to make sure he was heard over the deafening noise.

"*Six on number two, and two on three*," I replied adding, "T*hat's twelve... with us four here.*"

"That's what I count," Jenkins said, more to himself than as a

response to me. I could see he was working on the deployment of his rather short manned platoon. It all had to be worked out before we arrived: worked out, that is, to his meticulous satisfaction. However, rescue missions never gave us much time for strategy or thinking about risk analysis. We frequently went into an LZ that was hot and crawling with nasty little guys with hatred in their hearts.

Basically, we were firemen rushing into a burning building with helpless people inside. Only our buildings happened to be the jungle and the fires were lead bullets looking for a target. The people we looked to rescue, more than likely, were shot up or hurt from the crash and still in danger for something we feared more than death…being captured.

Still, on the way, you could see Blue's mind working out his strategy for the twelve of us; what formation we should take, and how to react to what might be waiting for us.

"*Ritchason make it?*" Blue asked about his platoon sergeant.

"*He's on two, with Adkins and Melton,*" I yelled back to let him know we had at least two M-60 machine gunners along. Spec 4 Kelly Adkins and PFC 3 Mike Melton came over shortly after I arrived and had already proven to be excellent machine gunners.

"*And Dornellas and Winship are in three,*" I added to inform him about the two experienced pointmen.

Blue sat in his usual position on the floor with his back resting against the door gunner's seat. It put him into position to be the first off the chopper and the last to get on. I typically sat across from him so the radio I carried was available for his use. My back rested against the co-pilot's seat and we both customarily had one leg hung over the side. He liked looking out the open door in the direction we were headed, and I had a good view of where we just came from.

As I looked back, the doorgunner was preparing for action by connecting several M-60 ammunition belts together, now filling several boxes. He put one end of the belt on his weapon, closed the cover and with a sharp blow of his wrist made sure it snapped into place. He then pulled back on the recoiling arm to load the first round.

Blue noticing the doorgunner's preparation, pulled an M-16 magazine out of his pouch and shoved it into his weapon. With his palm, he tapped the clip until it clicked. A click, so common to us by now, that we could hear it over the roar of the engines.

In one motion, Blue lifted his weapon off his lap, pointed it out the door and cocked it like he was shooting a bow and arrow. Without looking, he checked the safety switch with his thumb to make sure it was on and laid it back on his lap. It was then he noticed my M-16, which was already loaded and ready to go. It had a three-way magazine I just put together the day before with some electrician's tape. I tested the speed of changing clips with two clips facing up and one down. The three clips taped together increased my firing speed by double.

"*Where did you get that idea?*" Blue shouted to me, curious about my handiwork.

"*The movie... 'Hell is for Heroes,' with Steve McQueen*," I yelled back.

"*Did you test it?*"

"*Yes, yesterday, works bitchen!*" I said, and as an afterthought, "*I met him once.*"

"*Who, Steve McQueen*?" Blue said with a smile, and then looked back out over the jungle. The horrendous racket made all conversations short and to the point. Clouds were moving in quickly and more rain was on the way.

Off to our right, a few miles back, we could see three quick flashes of light that was followed a few seconds later by the deep and just barely discernible sound of 105 millimeter Howitzer cannon fire. A few seconds later we could see three light flashes about three miles out in front of us, and then the barely detectible crackling of the explosions.

Blue tapped the doorgunner's leg and asked him for the visitor's helmet. The gunner handed Blue the helmet that was hooked on the ceiling. The helmet was there for anyone who wanted to either listen to the pilots chattering on their intercom or to communicate with others in the general area. The noise prevented me from hearing what was being said. By his animated conversation, it was apparent Blue was trying to convince someone he needed something done and quickly. His conversation stopped and he looked back at the artillery base, which had discontinued their barrage.

Before long, we both could see a single flash. And, as before, several seconds later a flash appeared just ahead of us. Only this time the flash was further to the left of the previous target. It was a white marker-round that exploded about fifty feet above the dark jungle. There was more communication on Blue's part and then the full volley of artillery started up on what evidently was our soon to be LZ.

Blue had arranged to soften up the LZ just in case there were some non-friendlies still hanging around the area. Additionally, Blue arranged a series of quick target coordinates in the event we came under fire after hitting the landing zone and more artillery was needed.

"*Blue-India, remember Longshot one through four*," Blue informed me, so I could call in the Howitzers, if necessary. We had worked out a system on a clockwise rotation basis; one was north, two east, and so on. A quick call of "TA-4" (Target Area 4) to the artillery unit gave us a volley to the west of our position, and from there we could walk the artillery closer or further away.

The barrage on our LZ continued until our birds prepared to acquire their final approach. Two Charlie Troop choppers were already circling the LZ. A third, a LOACH, was off above a fire that was burning a couple of hundred meters in the jungle. Instinctively we knew what the fire was. We had seen it before; it was not a good sign.

Our pilots still flying in a "V" formation descended to the treetop level and reduced their speed slightly. The ride was now getting very bumpy as they maneuvered up and down to stay just barely above the different sized trees. Some branches hit the skids and others hit our scarred boots sticking out the door.

Near the LZ the pilots reduced their speed, dropped down into the grassy opening, and pushed up the nose like a cowboy rearing up his horse, to bring the bird to a halt over the touchdown area. Just before the skids hit the ground, the co-pilot turned on a spotlight, which let them measure the distance to the ground. He then quickly turned off the rather bright "*here I am, shoot me light*." The flash of brightness revealed the depth of the wind-brushed elephant grass and a few empty termite mounds that would make good cover.

The Blues prepared for their assault by standing on the landing-skids, taking their weapons off safety, and setting up to jump at the same time when the skids fleetingly touched the ground. It was a procedure we used quite frequently during the daylight; this was our first attempt into the bleak obscurity with all three birds landing at the same time.

The routine of stepping off must be completed simultaneously. The loss of several hundred pounds, on either side of the chopper, could easily throw off the pilot's control, sending the rotors into the ground or, worse yet, into another aircraft, killing all of us.

Our touchdown was subtle…but enough to give the Blues the signal to get off. The skids never came to rest on the grass. In a split second, and in one continuous motion, the birds were up in the air again. I was amazed at the soft touchdown in the darkness. It just showed the skill and talent of these Charlie Troop Cavalier pilots.

Our flying-horses quickly passed the treetops and the noise diminished into an eerie silence. The LZ was not hot, not a shot was fired while the birds were going in, always a good indication we had succeeded in landing in a quiet zone. The enemy loved shooting at aircraft, especially when they are hovering close to the ground.

"*Oh, Shit!*" I yelled, as I went head first into the wet muck. Unfortunately, the soft landing didn't help me. A few steps into the tall grass and, as usual, I was flat on my face. Not a bad practice when you're expecting a firefight, except this was just my usual clumsiness, facilitated by that fricking heavy radio and M-60 ammo I carried.

"*Blue-India is down again!*" was the standard remark and joke with the rest of the platoon. It didn't surprise me that Dornellas and some of the others were taking bets on how many times I would end up facedown during a mission.

I hoped the darkness had covered my fall and saved me from the usual ribbing. And it would have:

"*Oh, Shit!*" Yes, I went down a second time. This time tripped up by an abandoned termite mound that everyone else easily walked by.

"*That's two on landing,*" said Blue, "*I win the pot!*"

I couldn't believe even Cavalier Blue, my fearless leader, was placing bets on me falling down.

Only the sense of urgency kept everyone from making the usually embarrassing fuss over my ineptness. But you could still hear the low tone laughter from the rest. Truthfully, I enjoyed the attention; even laughing at myself helped relieve the tension.

Cavalier Blue swiftly gave orders to prepare to move out. Our Scoutbird had located a trail 20 meters off our target and he was ready to show us the way.

"*Cavalier Blue, this is Cav 22, come in,*" was the crackle I heard on my radio handset as I sat up. Cav 22 was a familiar voice of the well-liked WO Ernest Doom Burns, another New Yorker.

"*Cav 22, this is Blue-India, over.*"

"*Roger, India, your heading is to be 272 degrees, do you copy? Over.*"

"*Two-seven-two, that's a roger. Over,*" I responded. However, there was no real need for compass directions, the glow from the burning chopper gave us enough light to find our way to the trail.

"*Dornellas, take point, Winship back up,*" ordered Blue in a low tone, then looked my way and said, "*Blue-India, turn that damn volume down!*"

I was monitoring the radio on the way to the LZ and had turned the volume up to hear over the engine noise. I had forgotten to turn the volume down in the midst of hitting a pitch-black LZ and falling down twice.

Dornellas immediately found the trail. Upon Blue's hand signal, we moved out quickly and silently. The two-foot wide path made our passage through the jungle a great deal easier. The only need for a machete was the last twenty-feet or so, directly to the crash site.

The flapping of rotor-blades from our cover Pink Team, and the firefight which raged a few miles away at Firebase Dolly, covered any noise we did make. The base had been under attack for hours and the reason for one of our birds getting shot down. At first it was a fierce battle where the enemy succeeded in penetrating the barbed wire perimeter. But our gunships, artillery, and scout birds pushed back the strong contingent of NVA's. Our Cobras had silenced an NVA 82 mm mortars but not before they had inflicted some heavy casualties at the firebase.

When we reached our downed bird, the firefight at Dolly was down to sporadic bursts of heavy gunfire, exchanged at different parts of the perimeter. The enemy was continuously testing for weak spots in Dolly's defense.

When we moved closer to the fire, large sinister silhouettes reflected against the trees. Those shadows announced our presence to anyone within a couple hundred meters; only time would tell if some of the enemy broke off their attack to follow the helicopter they had shot down.

Between the downed LOACH and our entry point to the clearing, which was no more than 20 feet in width, was a pilot sitting against a rather large tree. His head was leaned back, a .45-caliber pistol was in his right hand, and his left hand rested on the body of his badly burned doorgunner. We could see from the track marks on the soft ground the pilot had dragged his crewman out of the chopper and away from the intense fire.

There was no sign of the co-pilot. The crew of an observation helicopter usually consists of two pilots and a spotter who also served as doorgunner, crew chief, and mechanic.

"*Don't fire, this is Cavalier Blue,*" Jenkins announced in a low voice, loud enough for the pilot to hear. There was no response.

"*We're friendlies. Don't fire*!" said Dornellas, who was the closest at this point. He turned to Blue, slowly shook his head, indicating he saw no movement and, with a tilted head and slowly closing his eyes, signaled that he thought he was a KIA.

"*Set up defensive positions,*" Blue whispered to Ritchason and pointed to indicate the distance he wanted his people from the chopper. The problem with the fire was there were grenades and other munitions, used by the doorgunner, which could still explode. Ammo discharging from a fire was unpredictable and just as dangerous as if fired out of a weapon.

Blue made his way closer to the downed officer, put his hand on the 45, to make sure if the pilot did move, there would be no accidental shooting, and then used his other hand to check for a pulse. I was kneeling in a defensive position a few feet away when Blue asked for the handset. His actions told me for certain we had two confirmed KIAs.

As Blue took the handset to make his call, I moved closer to the pilot and gently took the 45 out of the hand that was already showing signs of stiffening from rigor mortis. We were too late.

"*Cav 22, this is Cavalier Blue, come in, over,*" Blue said with a sullen tone.

"*Go ahead Blue, this is 22. Medivac is on its way!*" a hopeful response came.

"*Roger, we found two...still looking for number three, over,*" disclosed our platoon leader, getting ready to add the rest of the painful news.

"*Blue, this is 22, what is the status?*"

"*Cav 22,*" Blue started slowly, "*We need two ponchos, will advise on the third, over.*"

There was a silence as the message became clear to those listening. Ponchos meant bodybags. After what seemed like an eternity of deafening silence, the radio crackled again.

"*Cavalier Blue, this is Six, come-in,*" was the comeback, which perked Blue up to a more respectful posture. Cavalier Six was Major Thomas M. Felton, (KIA July 14, 1969 Panel 21W line 116) our company commander at that time.

"*Roger, Six, this is Blue, over.*"

"*Do I understand we have two confirmed? Is that correct?*" said the voice to get a clearer understanding.

"*Roger Six, that's confirmed. We're still searching for the other,*" Blue responded trying not to give too much information over a radio frequency that surely was being monitored by the enemy.

"*Make haste, Blue. You're not alone down there. Understood?*" Six said in a cautioning tone.

"*Roger, will do, Blue out!*" Blue turned to me with a look that would be repeated more times than either of us had hoped.

Sergeant Ritchason was busy with a long bamboo shaft he had cut down and was conducting the search for the missing co-pilot by prodding the pole in the middle of the smoldering fire. Our experience was few walked away from the crash and more than likely the body was still in the chopper's ashes. What's more, we could smell the horrifying odor of burning flesh, which came from the chopper's remains. It didn't take long for the bamboo pole to catch fire, but not before Ritchason had found a large rubbery object. A couple more prods and what was left of the third crewmember was pushed out of the fire. The only thing left was the rather large torso…no limbs…no skull.

Everyone was visibly disturbed at the sight, and the revolting smell sickened a couple of new guys. We avoided looking into each other's eyes; afraid of what emotions we might see. The thought of placing the KIA into a bag was hard to stomach. It was a task that did not become easier no matter how often we had to execute it.

"*Cavalier Six, this is Blue, come in, over,*" he called up to his commanding officer. You could see the disheartened look in Blue's face and hear his normally emotionless radio voice full of vacillating unevenness.

"*Roger Blue, this is Six, what's your sit-rep?*"

"*Found number three, need three ponchos,*" Blue answered with minimal chatter. He tossed the handset to me, walked over to Blue-Mike to discuss how to move us back to the LZ. Blue then came back, radioed his intentions to walk the KIAs back to the LZ to Six, and then sat down beside me.

"*So, where did you meet Steve McQueen?*" he said, trying to change the somber mood. There was really nothing more we could do, and thinking about the lives that had just been lost would do us no good on future missions. Blue knew that. He also was good at maintaining his platoon's emotional stress at an acceptable level. It's strange how quickly the mind can temporarily shut out unwanted thoughts.

It took an inordinate amount of time to make our way back to the LZ.

Dornellas stood in the middle and signaled our flying coaches with a stroblight. The three birds ascended as quickly as they had landed, only this time it seemed everything was moving in slow motion. Leaving an LZ was always the most nerve-racking. The last thing any of us wanted was to get shot as we were completing a mission.

On the way back to Phouc Vinh our thoughts were on those who had just died. Sitting beside American KIAs who were deferentially placed into an inhospitable bodybag creates a ghost that must be battled at another time…and another place.

Downed Fixed Wing

Lt. Glenn Jenkins settled into the Blue Annihilators or more correctly we molded ourselves into the Buddha Blues. He was respected by his fellow officers and NCOs and provided the Blues the kind of leadership needed to minimize casualties and yet still be very productive in the missions set before us. Frequently we were inserted quickly to recon an area and quickly pulled out. Blue viewed our missions as information gathering, not as a gung-ho first strike force. Our days, during this time, were spent waiting for missions, which would provide the ground troops an enemy they could quickly engage.

One particular day we sat on a dirt road for a couple of hours waiting for such a recon mission.

"Hey, some guy is looking for you over there," Lt. Jenkins informed me. We were close to another unit who also was waiting by the road.

"Must be Duffy," I said, knowing the only guy out in the jungle who would be looking for me; except the enemy maybe. As I was about to get up to look for my friend, I was tapped on the shoulder.

"What's hanging, Tom?" Duffy said, looking down at me with that big surfer smile. He was shirtless, quite tan, and had a beach towel around his neck.

"Hey, Duffy, good to see ya, man,"

"What are you guys doing here," he asked and I told him, *"Just hanging 'til our next mission."* It was funny because the last card I got from him was about going together on R & R in Australia in September.

"Did you book the R & R?" I asked

"No, I was waiting to see when you wanted to make it," he responded.

"How about the third week in September?"

"Sounds good to me," Duffy said and told me he would let me know what hotel he would book.

"Blues, pack up! We're off again," Blue-Mike announced.

"See ya later, Duffy, R & R in Sidney, bitchin'... man," I told him, as I put my gear on and loaded my magazine into my M16.

Duffy started to walk down the road with the towel still around his neck and I wondered how he got a beach towel and stayed so tan out here in the jungle. Then, just before I hopped on the chopper, I remembered I had my camera with me.

"Hey, Duffy," I yelled, but with the chopper blades grinding up he couldn't hear me. So, the shot in my scrapbook is of Duffy about fifty feet down the road walking away. We went to Sydney as planned, but that's another X rated story.

"We have a downed fixed wing aircraft," Blue told us as we boarded.

"Fixed wing, wow, that's a new one," Blue-Mike said, *"Is that why we're not on a rushed Downed Bird Call?"*

"Yeah, not much movement was spotted from the air, so we need to go in to find the crew."

The aircraft was a C 130 with seven on board. It was taking off from Ben Hoa about 30 miles away and crashed into an open rice patty area we had used as an LZ before.

"Things don't look good," Blue said, as we stepped off the chopper.

"We're going to have to wait and let this fire burn down before we can retrieve anybody," Ritchason told us, as he ordered the rest of the Blues to form a defensive perimeter. He and Dornellas started looking through parts of the plane that were not fiercely burning.

"There are two over here," Dornellas said, as he pointed to a main section, which looked like parts of the cockpit. He was right; it was the pilot and co-pilot.

"*Blue-India, help me with this one,*" Blue-Mike called to me as he was trying to carry another officer out of the plane. Blue suggested he must have been the navigator.

Soon we had six of the seven in bodybags.

"*Cavalier 17, this is Blue-India, come in.*" I called for our UH-1Hs so we could load those we had found and have them airlifted to Ben Hoa.

"*This is 17, have you found all?*" was the response.

"*That's a negative, still looking for one more.*" I advised knowing the last crewmember must be somewhere in the midst of the biggest flames.

"Ask them, are they sure of the number?" Blue told me to pass on to Cav 17.

"*Cav 17, are we certain we have a correct number of crewmembers?"*

"*Wait one, I'll check.*"

A few minutes passed while Ritchason and Dornellas continued to look around the wreckage. There was nothing else to be found without going right in the middle of the blistering fuselage and that part was just too hot to get anywhere within ten feet. It was apparent the fire was going to last for some time and the afternoon Monsoons were looking very threatening. Heavy thunderclouds were moving in quickly. The word was a big storm was expected to hit, which would keep our birds grounded for the next couple of days.

"What do think, Blue?" Ritchason asked about whether we should continue the search or head back.

"Let's see if the number is right...keep on looking," he said, concerned about spending the night out near this fire that would be visible for miles.

"Blue-India, this Cavalier 17, come in."

"Go ahead 17, do we need to look further?" I asked, hoping the count was off by one and we could head back.

"We're short one?" Blue asked me and I nodded.

"Keep on searching. We're not leaving until we find him," was the answer. We knew Blue would not leave anyone behind even if we had to

search all night.

Blue-Mike had found a lengthy piece of pipe from one of the wing sections, which had a 90-degree angle on the end and started to prod in the midst of the biggest flames. The main fire was about 20 feet across and at least 10 feet wide, more than likely burning up most of the plane's fuel.

"I got something," Ritchason declared as he felt a soft mass with the pipe. He prodded some more and was able to hook the end of the pipe to whatever the soft mass was.

"Got number seven," Blue announced. He picked up another pipe and they both forced the body away from the fire.

"Cav 17, this is Blue-India, we found the last one, please call for pickup." I advised our cover birds to get our transports ASAP.

"Let's turn him over," Blue told Ritchason. As they did, you could finally recognize there was a body. The strange thing was the bottom was not burned. You could see the green uniform and in the pants pocket was a wallet.

"Look, the wallet is intact," Dornellas said, and pulled out a couple of hundred dollar bills and a Playboy Membership card. We hadn't seen US dollars since we came to Nam. The currency we had to use was Vietnamese Script, and the dollars told us the C-130 had originated from outside the country.

"*Put it back*," Blue told the sergeant, "*Let's get the bag and get out of here.*"

"Birds are on final approach," I told Blue, after I received the call from Cav 17.

The bodybag was put on our bird and the rest of the Blues crammed into the other two transports. I know we all were thinking about the C-130 crewmember and how little there was left of him. His ID in his wallet said he was 6 ft 2 inches, but all we bagged was about four feet.

"Hold on, guys, this is going to be rocky," the door gunner passed on the message from the pilot as we tried to fly around a thunderstorm ahead. We were about 300 feet above the treetops when the storm's heaviest winds hit us. Within seconds we were at treetop level sideways looking straight

down at the ground.

Blue grabbed Dornellas who was halfway out of the chopper and I grabbed the bodybag that was also heading out. Not too happy with heights and hanging out of the open doors, I used a repelling shackle attached to my ammo belt and hooked it to the floor of the chopper. Thoughts of falling out in midair made me cautious.

Our pilot straightened the bird as the heavy deluge hit the windshield, in effect, making both pilots blind. Both door gunners had some visibility and helped guide the chopper out of the thunderhead.

"That's enough fun for today," Blue commented, when we exited the chopper back at Phouc Vinh. The bird then again took off to deliver the body to Ben Hoa.

"I don't envy those guys having to fly in this weather," Ritchason stated.

"Yes, but the guy deserves to be with the rest of his crew," Blue acknowledged. We knew if he were flying that chopper, he would make the trip regardless of the weather.

Search Continues

As with Duffy and Blue-Mike, I mailed letters to Glenn Jenkins in the Ohio area with no success. One response came back by e-mail:

<*Tom, sorry that I'm not the Glenn Jenkins you are looking for. I was in the Navy back in1973-1975. I never had to serve in the Pacific (Vietnam), Good Luck. Glenn A. Jenkins, Ironton, Ohio.*>

I made several phone calls to G. Jenkins in Cleveland with no luck. Our chatroom e-mail correspondence went something like this:

<*Still Searching for Buddha Jenkins*>

<*We have addresses on almost 400 troopers but the list is getting smaller as folks move and don't keep us in the net. We do not have contact data for Glenn A Jenkins. I wish we did. A good man. Maybe Walker Jones can put out a call to the 1st Cav Association to see if anyone can locate him. I spend some time in AZ each year. Maybe we can connect. Cheers.* Bob>

<*Hi, I was Blue-India in 1971 and I have addresses for some of the*

Blues. I got to the 1/9 C troop on Jan 3, 1971. I still have orders with all the Blues names from Nam. BI 71>

<Great BI 71, any info for 69 & 70 will be appreciated. I'm still trying to get an address on Cav Blue, Buddha Jenkins. Trying to contact as many Blues as I can. Talked with Staff Sgt Gary Ritchason and he is doing well in the Chicago area, does not like computers so he won't chat. Any other Blue contacts of the 69/70 era contact me; I'm trying to make a list. Thanks, BI 69>

<Hey, I do remember Jenkins telling me he was going to open a combination massage parlor, house of Ill repute, and bar in Cleveland when he got back to the world. He was talking crazy like that toward the end of his tour. I know I got a little crazy after running around with the Blues. So it's understandable. I can see him now, head bald except a long pigtail down his back with a big Manchu mustache, rings on all fingers, shoes that turn up at the toes. Smoking big cigars. Big Tattoos all over. Coulda happened. --Cavalier Blue 1970>

<Roger that, I guess we have to get the old beads out and start communications with Buddha about Buddha Jenkins. I mailed a letter to Glen Jenkins in Ohio, got one response. If we had an area I could widen the search by sending a search for a relative letter. Thanks, BI 69.>

<TC, Now Blue 70 thinks both of us are full of Crap and he's probably right. Ref: Buddha Jenkins, never heard from him after our SE Asia vacation. I went to http://www.military.com - they have a "find a buddy" section – found a Glenn Allen Jenkins, Army, Rank 03 (Capt), MOS 1981 – Helicopter Pilot – but if you search Ohio, there are about 3 or 4 Glenn Jenkins in different towns – search US and a lot more. That's a start. Maybe you already have done that. I'll check my orders and see if I have any SSN or Army ID number – Saber Six, out>

The last e-mail we received reassured us that Buddha Jenkins was still running amuck in 1979:

To: ctrp9thcav@yahoogroups.com

From: renasdayspa@

Date: Sat, 3 May 2008 18:40:03 EDT

Subject: Re: [ctrp9thcav] Still searching

Tom, John

Last time I saw him, he was Major Jenkins. We were in the 3rd Armored Div in 77-79 together. As you said, the stories :-)! He hadn't changed a bit since Nam. We went on a Rhine River Cruise and he almost got me and himself kicked off the boat. If they could have stopped the boat we would have been off.

Russ—Cavalier 14

The search for Glenn A. (Buddha) Jenkins, Freeman (Duffy) Daugherty, and others continues, however, the more time that passes, the more I fear something happened to these bigger-than-life heroes of Vietnam.

At times, when I travel, a scene plays in my mind that one day someone would tap me on the shoulder and say, "Don't I know you?" And it happens to be Duffy or Buddha. Or I envision what you see in movies, two people looking for each other and passing by each other in an airport not knowing how close they came to seeing each other again.

We experienced war together, had plenty of laughs, and now I wish we could talk once more. Our memories of events would differ and each would remember different events. One thing for certain…we all buried our Ghosts in a closet and some may never recover or wish to open the closet door again. All I can do is hope they are safe, are not battling Agent Orange diseases or PTSD, and have the happy and full life they deserve.

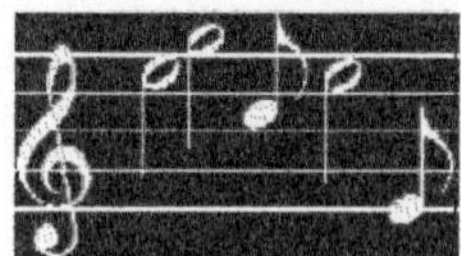

VI..ET..N..AM...VI..ET..N..AM

LATE AT NIGHT WHILE YOU'RE SLEEPING

Chapter VIII – Families Want to Open The Closet Door

Julie Kink – In honor and memory of her big brother.

One day, just after the turn of the new century, we received an amazing and wonderful e-mail from a young woman who was inquiring about her older brother. She had contacted the president and every governmental agency she could think of to find out more about what happened to him. She was frustrated, had found very little information, and her search was going nowhere.

I was really touched when I saw the picture she sent us. It showed herself at 7 years old, her mother proudly standing with two of her children, and her tall handsome brother in uniform. She wanted to find out more about his tour, those who served with him, and the men who died with him in a helicopter. She now is our Little Sis. She finally found the brothers of her brother.

I e-mailed Julie just after a reunion of the Vietnam Helicopter Pilot Association (VHPA) in San Antonio and asked her if I could include some of the e-mails, which passed through our chat-group. But I found she can tell her story best and the following is a speech she gave at the Vietnam Women's Memorial on Veteran's Day 2000.

"I've only seen one aviator killed since I've been here," my brother wrote in his last letter home, July 14, 1969. He had been in Vietnam for 3 weeks, and was trying to reassure mom.

'You see, you're never alone on a mission. There's always somebody to protect you and get you out even before you hit the ground. I just don't want you to

get upset because if you go down, you're only on the ground for about 3 minutes before they get you out of the area. We have what they call a downed bird alarm in all of the hootches. Whenever a bird goes down every bird here is airborne and enroute to provide assistance in less than 2 minutes. So you see there's really nothing to worry about.'

A week after he wrote that, David was flying as observer in a light observation helicopter that was brought down by a secondary explosion. The pilot, John Anderson and gunner, Edward Dennull, were killed. David died 12 days later on August 3.

He was 19.

I was seven the day Mom, Dad and I saw David off at Truax field in Madison, Wisconsin on the way to Vietnam. I remember it being one of those days when cameras are hauled out reluctantly and clicked only once or twice, because of the wind or the sun or the awkwardness of the moment. One black and white Polaroid survived from that day: my mom smiling, heroically grasping two of her kids, me resentful of her hand clamping my shoulder . . . and my brother David, tall and proud in his "dress" tans, with a mustache that looked pasted on, but still gave him that slightly older look he was after.

I had just turned 8 a month later, the night my teenage sister called my oldest brother over to the house, and they talked in hushed voices in the dining room about a telegram until Mom got home from work. What followed changed my family and my life.

My mom cried and fought hard to get more details from the Army, Dad grieved silently, and my older brother and sister never talked about it. I learned that the Vietnam War was a subject that brought out strong and frightening emotions, a subject better left alone.

So the years went by, and the name "David" came to mean a marker in a cemetery; an insignia and some medals; the musty, overseas smell I will never forget, associated forever with the strange words, "personal effects"; a box of military letters and papers; and a few photos. Each time I stared into the face in those photos, I tried so hard to remember the tone of his voice, how long his fingers were, how his jacket felt. But I couldn't.

For many years, I wondered what it would be like to be 19 and piloting a helicopter, 19 and fighting a war, 19 and dying. No one talked about David, and in fact most of my best friends never knew I lost a brother in Vietnam. I longed to find out more about him. I just didn't know how.

After years of wanting to find people who knew David, in 1993 I wrote a letter to the President of the United States, asking for help obtaining information. The response was a form letter and a fee schedule for records search; so I chose a different path.

That September, I visited "The Moving Wall" and registered with the Friends of the Vietnam Veterans Memorial's "In Touch" program. The following February, I received my first response.

Chris McGorman wrote that he may have known my brother. I knew I had to call him but I was nervous, partly because I was afraid he hadn't known David, and partly due to the stereotype of Vietnam veterans I had inherited from Hollywood.

Chris had not known my brother, but talking with him opened up a whole new world. A few days later, I received another letter from him, with advice on where to continue my search, a membership directory of the First Cav Division Association, and a First Cav pin.

Chris wrote in part, "Your brother was in one of the finest outfits in the finest Army division during that war. I know he was proud to be in C Troop 1st Squadron 9th Cavalry, and you should be proud of that fact as well. I feel confident you'll find your brother's friends . . . David would be proud to have a sister like you."

I spent hours going through the 1st Cav directory, and came up with the names of eight men who would have been in David's unit during the time he served. I sent letters, hoping at least one would write back. Two came back with no forwarding address. One of the men called, two wrote back with additional sources of information and encouragement. But none of them had known David.

In 1996, I found the Vietnam Helicopter Crew Members Association and Pilots Association, and the Vietnam Helicopter Flight Crew Network, an Internet group of 350 former helicopter crew members. It brought tears to my eyes when one of them wrote, 'Your brother was our brother.' That man is standing back there. Jim Schueckler . . . thank you.

I began receiving emails from pilots sharing memories of their time with the 1st Cav and other units that were tightly organized and dedicated to each other. Doug Ashworth wrote, 'Yes, Julie, there is a great deal of camaraderie and a sense of brotherhood among the helicopter pilots who flew in Vietnam. But there is an even stronger tie between the pilots who flew in the 1st of the 9th. We all knew, if we went down, every single crewmember back at the hootch had only one mission in life, and that was to get to us as quickly as possible. What your brother was a part of gives you much to be proud of. Being a LOH pilot in Charlie troop makes him my brother too.'

At last, after searching for three years for someone who knew David, I was contacted by a buddy of his from flight school. Jon Harris told me about learning to fly, teasing on the bus on the way to the flight line, and the jokes they played on each other. At last I was hearing the stories I never got a chance to hear.

Then, the day after Christmas, 1996, I received a letter from the first person from David's unit and time period to contact me. John Powell wrote, *'It's difficult to lose friends because the guys in C troop were closer than that, the bonds formed in combat are in many ways stronger than family. The day your brother went down, I was flying Cobra cover and was there until he was recovered. I never knew what* happened to him until now.*'* John Powell . . . thank you.

On August 3, 1997, 28 years to the day after David died, I received my first phone call from Bob Tredway, his troop commander who had the humbling task of writing my family condolences back in 1969. Bob Tredway . . . thank you. I've met Luther Russell, who flew to the crash site and helped put David on the Medivac. And I've finally met David's best friend from flight school and Charlie Troop, Steve Karas, whose name I have known since I was eight years old.

I've been given many opportunities to help other family members trying to find people who knew their loved one who died in Vietnam. In 1997, I was allowed to join the Internet flight crew network, and the Family Contacts Committee was formed to help bring family members and friends of helicopter casualties together. As a committee, the 8 of us have helped with more than 250 cases. We draw on the VHPA, VHCMA, internet groups and other resources to find veterans willing to share their memories with the families and friends of the fallen.

The clarity, insight and depth of emotion in nearly every veteran who crosses my path astounds me. And I have been told, over and over again, that the connection brings a welcome kind of peace to the veterans, too.

One former pilot wrote to a brother of a KIA, "I have never forgotten your brother - he died for me. Milt freely took my place as a favor in an aircraft that had five more minutes left before it took good men to their graves. At the time, I was a married man with a 6-month old son. That boy grew up with a father thanks to Milt; he is now a Captain in the Army (soon to be Major). I am glad to finally be able to tell someone about how I was spared because another stepped up to take my place," he wrote.

A veteran once posed a question that made me think. What do you get out of these connections, going to the reunions, being at the Wall? My answer, always evolving, is that it allows David to grow up. For all those years before I ever knew what a Vietnam helicopter pilot looked like, talked like, felt like, my only reference was a brother I never really knew . . . and what movies and the media told me. Now, my "new big brothers" have shown me what David might be like today.

How many of you are Vietnam Veterans? You are the only ones who can fill in the blanks, for people like me. Being with veterans, for us, draws a parallel between then and now. Only through you guys, can the lost ones grow up. They cannot do it themselves anymore. Only on the backs of their friends, as surely as their arms were slung over your shoulders in another time and place, can they be carried forward. You are the bridge. Please remember that. Don't let a day go by without having a little bit of fun, for them. And stand proud, because you are a Vietnam Veteran.

Thinking about my search and the extraordinary people it has brought into my life, I remember sitting in a tenth grade history classroom and realizing for the first time ever that I was part of a generation that was dying, as all generations are, really, from the moment they are born. Perhaps some of you had that feeling a long time ago in Vietnam. I realize that someday, the reunions will end, the hugs and tears and laughter and closeness that is celebrated among you guys, will be gone.

But what was shared here, with each other and with family members of our fallen brothers, will not be forgotten. By your presence here today, you have brought a part of our brothers, uncles, sons, husbands, and dads back to us. Perhaps the greatest gift we families can give you, in return, is to say, 'Welcome Home.' The fact *that each of you is here today is a miracle, and an indication of the larger pattern that we can only glimpse.*

I see reflections of that "larger pattern" in the scribblings of a 19-year-old kid who already knew, after just 3 weeks in The Cav, 'You're never alone on a mission.' *In closing I want to share a quote attributed to Maj. Michael David O'Donnell at Dak To, January 1, 1970.*

'If you are able, save for them a place inside of you and save one backward *glance when you are leaving for the places they can no longer go. Be not ashamed to say you loved them though you may or may not have always. Take what they have left and what they have taught you with their dying, and keep it with your own, and in that time when men decide and feel safe to call the war insane, take one moment to embrace those gentle heroes you left behind.*

Thank you. Julie Kink, Little Sis"

Over the years, Julie has been a great part of our communications network and honestly has become our "Little Sis." We all were recently sorrowed by the loss of her mother that she shared with us and we hope, being part of Charlie Troop, it made her understand we shared in her loss.

Julie continues to work fervently with family members who want to find out more about those who served. She is also frequently seen at reunions, usually busy helping some lost soul or a family member who is trying to find their way around.

The dedication she put into being a greater part of her brother's life is exemplary and there could be no greater honor for David Kink than to know his little sister has become Charlie Troop's "Big Little Sis."

Her latest e-mail read:

From: kink100@
Date: Mon, 21 Jul 2008 00:31:56 +0000
Subject: [ctrp9thcav] 39 years

It's hard to believe it's been 39 years since July 21, 1969. The day man first walked on the Moon. The day LOH 67-16566 crashed due to a ground explosion from a camouflaged US bomb that was fired upon. The day our families' lives changed.

WO1 John E. Anderson KIA - age 20 - an officer's son from Fort Benning, (Panel 20W line 27)

SP4 Edward Michael Dennull KIA - age 18 - a farm boy from a large Ohio family. (Panel 20W line 28)

WO1 David R. Kink WIA - age 19, DOI 8-3-1969 - an immigrant's son from Wisconsin whose ambition was to learn to fly.

(Panel 20W line 92)

Thank you all for helping me get to know my brother David, through you.

Little sister, Julie Kink

Fritz Miller – In honor of his Uncle Bill Potter

We received an e-mail from Julie one day introducing us to Fritz Miller. He was searching for information about his uncle William D. Potter. Fritz was like many family members who had searched for more information, but was continuously running into a dead end. That is, until he found Julie and the 1/9th chatgroup.

After years of following leads he was able to piece together, Fritz came back just recently with one of the most detailed and comprehensive reports on his uncle and those men who served with him. I was still an FNG when the helicopter was shot down that had five soldiers aboard and my memory was extremely sketchy. It would have been one of my first rescue missions and, as an FNG, things were so new and strange; the memory was just a flash. I do know there was a great deal of talk about a bird that had been shot down and the NVA was trying to bring in more heavy anti-aircraft weapons.

Finally, when I was able to read the report, I was overwhelmed by the details he was able to discover. I know he dedicated many years to his search and by doing so honored the memory of his uncle. He was able to chronicle his uncle's military tour and many of the pilots he trained with and later served in Vietnam.

He described how fellow student pilots in Potter's class wanted to go to the best unit and fly with the best pilots. Their inquiry from returning Vietnam Veteran pilots was that the 1st of the 9th was on top of the list. In one part he wrote, "Of the 17 men who made the pact to join the 1st of the 9th, 10 didn't complete their tour; they were either killed or wounded."

He did send us this e-mail thank you:

From: *"Fritz Miller" overfork@t*
To: *tlcriser@yahoo.com*
Subject: *how are things?*
Date: *Mon, 26 May 2008 21:46:15 -0500*

Tom,
I've been on the road...sorry for taking so long to get back with you.
I can't tell you how much I appreciate your communication with me. After the call went out looking for people who might have known my uncle, you were the first who replied. I'm sure that however many times you talk about it and think about it, you must have had second thoughts before contacting me. I'm so glad you did.

Through the good work of your comrades, and the fine people at the Family Contacts Committee - particularly Julie Kink - I have been in contact with a number of men who served with my uncle, Bill Potter in C/1/9.

I also made contact with three of the men whom my uncle considered his closest friends in flight school. In July of 2006 I was on vacation in Washington, D.C. with my family, while at the same time a reunion of the Vietnam Helicopter Pilot's Association met. So, I met these guys. They shared stories with me about my uncle and helped me understand, to their best ability, what my uncle had meant to them. It was a cathartic experience. I am still in touch with them via email and letter.
Through much research and the willingness of people to communicate, I have found much out about my uncle's service. I have also made contact with the family members of 3 of the other 4 men who were also killed when their helicopter was downed. I was thrilled to learn much about the background of Bard "Lurch" Davenport, "Little" John Waller, and Lt. Brent Bell. I have written much about what I've discovered. I will attempt to send it to you under separate cover - it might be too large for this email.

Again, I want to say thanks to you for helping me in my quest. As a result, when I remember my uncle on days like today, I have a much deeper understanding of not only what he did during the war, but of how he was truly surrounded by friends and comrades. And I give thanks for your service, as well. I hope you had a good Memorial Day.

Fritz Miller overfork@

And my response:

Fritz,
I finally got the time to reread your story and take it in. Lots of great pictures and you most certainly did a great reporter's job; guess you learned it from the TV business. Details are amazing. By the way, the picture of the Hootch that was hit and roof was caved in was the Blues and my introduction to nightly rockets. I was only there a week or two when that happened. We used to get up at 1am because we knew we would get hit. We all sat in a bunker next door and waited for it to be over. One of the short-timers decided not to go into the bunker, the rocket hit right on top of him, his back was covered with shrapnel. Four of us took him to the medic tent, while the rockets were still going off. We were pissed at him because of putting us in danger just because he didn't get up and walk 20 ft. He was sent home. Forgot his name but not that night. I can't believe you got a picture of that.
Later, Tom

The picture I mentioned in the e-mail was quite a revelation. I didn't know it existed. Needless to say, it brought a rush of memories of that night and the early days of my time in Nam. I had retained the fun memories of beer parties, poker games, and volleyball matches. I had erased the nightly rocket attacks and especially pushed the night we got hit deep into my closet.

Fritz expressed how the Vietnam era impacted his family, "*It was a confusing time for families like ours. Soldiers who died in Vietnam were described as being 'wasted.' Our family wanted the war to end so that other families wouldn't have to mourn the loss of their son, brother or uncle, but we wanted the men who served their country to be able to come home with their heads held high.*"

Here is part of his report and dedication to those who died at the same time as Bill Potter:

On the 27th of March 1969 UH-1H tail number 66-16714 was lost to hostile fire at XT 636587 in Binh Long Province, Republic of Viet Nam. Killed that day were four aircrew from C Company, 1st SQ, 9th Cavalry and one passenger:
WO1 Bard Elton Davenport, pilot -- Panel 28W line 058
Sgt Allan G. Harper, air crewman -- Panel 28W - Row 060
SP5 John Bussey Waller, air crewman – Panel 28W - Row 064
1Lt William Brent Bell, H Co, 75th Inf (Rangers) -- Panel 28W Line 057
Warrant Officer Potter arrived in Vietnam on Saturday, 15 March 1969; he died on Thursday, 27 March 1969
WO 1 William Don Potter virtual wall URL
(http://www.virtualwall.org/dp/PotterWD01a.htm)

More Contacts from Family Members

The most rewarding part of our webpage and chatroom, which all the credit has to go to Jack Schwarz and Walker Jones, is the contacts from family members. Just a few weeks ago we received an inquiry from Major Tom Felton's brother. He wrote in an e-mail:

From: lovedixie2@>
Subject: Re: Re: Fw: Re: Tom Felton, C Troop Commander, KIA 1969
To: cavaliertex@
Date: Wednesday, July 30, 2008, 5:01 AM

I have located a portion of Tom's flight records: April 1961 thru June 1969. This record has his personal signature on it. The record shows he had a total of 3,399 hours military flying time. Of which 973 were combat time. For the month of June '69, he had a total of 65.2 hours: 26.8 in an AH-1G and 38.4 in a UH-1B. Of those 65.2 hours: 50.9 as Aircraft Commander and 14.3 as First Pilot. [I don't know what the difference is.] As of this date, 29 July 2008, I have been unable to locate his flight records for July 1-14, 1969. Thus, my belief that he had over 1,000 Combat hours. I may have mentioned this to you earlier, that his Air Medal has 39 Oak Leaf Clusters. Which, if I have been correctly instructed, amounts to 1,000 combat hours.

How do these hours compare to other pilots, troop commanders, squadron leaders, etc.? Please, somebody, I need a reference point?

This is part of the response from a fellow Cavalier:

<The Troop Operations Officer had put a red "NO FLY" grease pen circle on the AO Ops map, near LZ Dolly. Felton asked what that was for and was told that was where the previous CO's LOACH had been shot down by a .51 cal machine gun, so the "NO FLY" circle was to keep guys from flying into the area. Felton told him to take the "NO FLY" circle off the map and to include the information in the briefing to all pilots flying around the area, that we were the 1st of the 9th and we went wherever we wanted to go; if there was an enemy anti-aircraft gun there we would take it out, not leave it alone!

Felton did not say it with bravado, he was just businesslike and matter-of-fact. I rarely saw him angry, or heard him raise his voice in anger or frustration. He was always courteous to everyone and I never heard him be otherwise.

Physically he was short; I'm short, but I looked down at him. However, in all my time in both the Marines (before the war) and later in the Army, I never served under a commander I respected more -- a couple of them rated right up there with him, but none higher.>

Family members who search for more information and seek to find closure get the straight story from the brothers of their lost ones. This kind of response has to enthrall the searchers and let them know the honor which we hold for our lost Cavaliers. We receive "thank you" e-mails all the time stating that the information was very helpful and permitted them to close a chapter knowing their loss was not in vain.

At times, I do wish inquiries would come from White, Carroll, or Dornellas' families so I could tell them the kind of heroes they were and that they should be very proud. They honored America with their exemplary behavior as soldiers and they died heroes.

Chaplain Newby, in his two books, summed it up very neatly,

"It took Heroes!"

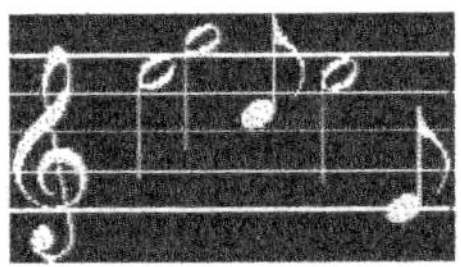

CHARLIE KONG COMES A CREEPIN ALL AROUND

Chapter IX – Parading Warriors

In the beginning of this book, I mentioned the parades in Thousand Oaks and what my impression was of those who participated. The media clearly influenced me as it did so many others at that time. As it turned out, one of those parading Vets and the one responsible for bringing the traveling Vietnam wall to the area was Forrest Frields.

He was in Charlie Troop in 1968 and '69, left Nam a few weeks before I joined the Blues. He was a Scout pilot with the handle of Cavalier White 11. Additionally, he was a solid member of the Thousand Oaks community, and owner of Forrest Photography. We actually met on many occasions doing volunteer work. Neither suspecting we had served in the same places, with the same unit, and knew some of the same people.

Each year more and more Vietnam Vets joined the parade until they consisted of a compliment of 20 to 25. In 1992, after the 1st Gulf War, the parade took on a more patriotic theme. More flags were being waved and an increase in the pride of our troops was apparent.

What was amazing, and sent chills down everyone's spine, was the welcome the Vietnam Vets were now getting. The sizable crowd stood up and applauded with enthusiasm as the guys marched past. At first it was just a polite applause and a few cheers.

However, by 1994, my last parade in Thousand Oaks, the applause was tremendous, and the cheers truly heartfelt. The Vietnam Warriors had come out of the closet to long delayed cheers and a true welcome home.

When Forrest and I finally met as Cavalier Brothers it was both a thrill and an embarrassment for me. I am a Vietnam Veteran who had the same negative image the media so successfully burned into the minds of Americans.

Was part of the reason so many put The Ghost in their closets because they were embarrassed to be considered one of them? How many others did the same thing…hide from the truth and unceremoniously stuffed their heroism into an emotional bodybag?

E-mail from Forrest Frields:

From:"Forrest"

To:"Tom Criser Blue-India"

Subject: Our meet

Date: Sun, 18 Jan 2004 07:28:06 -0800

Tom - it was my pleasure to meet you Friday night at the Crown and Anchor. The restaurant came before us when I was on the Planning Commission for something - I forget what. But there after, a couple of us commissioners would drop into the place for a late night "banger" and a beer.

I've attached an email that I sent out the next AM to some close friends about our encounter…

Last evening I met with a gent that I've been corresponding with via email for a couple of years.

He now lives in Corpus Christi, Texas formerly of Thousand Oaks formerly of the First Cav formerly of the 1st of the Ninth formerly of "C" troop of the 1/9th Cav - my first RVN tour unit!

We didn't serve together back then - we missed each other by two months but we were in the same unit with the same mission, etc.

What a rush! The war stories were fast and furious, inflated and bullshit! It was great! Tom Criser was the radio operator for our "Blue" (infantry) platoon. We have mutual friends who live here in TO who introduced us after he moved to Corpus in 1994 - an Irish fellow named Irish John Gore; Paul & Marty Campbell; Bob Rickards, etc.

I came home filled with piss and vinegar. Tom brought his First Cav "Recon" tattoo on his arm; I wore my cameo Cav patch on my shirt and my real First Cav Stetson - both with 1/9th original brass!

I'm still wondering what was so special about my tour with the Cav that was so special to me that I'm so proud to have served....

Even now as I pause to read what I've written to you I choke and tear up with emotion recalling those days so long ago filled with adventure, death, thrill and fear -my other life; so different from this one and yet so shared with you.

Such must be the price for old men to pay.....

Forrest

Forrest's e-mail is a tribute to those who didn't succumb to the media and stood in honor against the crowd. It seems we all had to find a reason for the war and resolve issues that were so negative, at one time, into a more pragmatic and acceptable point of view. The Vietnam War, contrary to popular myths, impacted this country in many favorable ways.

One of the most important aspects was the war tested this country's resolve to the importance of Freedom of Speech. What other country could survive such tumultuous years and still stay united? The Soviet Union could not! Most other countries would have had revolutions or numerous assassinations. Not the United States of America.

We are a young country who had its Civil War. That war strengthened this country even though there were massive casualties (600,000 KIAs). All countries need time to mature and find their way in the world. It's not any different than young adults growing to maturity. Our leaders needed time to mature after the Civil War...as this country has done after the Vietnam War.

Those 58,195 names on the Vietnam Wall served this country with honor and pride. They may not have agreed with the reasons for the war or with some of its leaders, but it was and still is an honor to serve and, yes, die for the country you love.

This war also changed how our military was to conduct future conflicts and how to better take care of its soldiers. In WWII many of the newest, youngest, and least trained were thrown to the front lines with expectations of high casualties. Not in Vietnam. In Nam, our soldiers were within 30 minutes of extensive medical care. Medics worked miracles under fire, Medivac pilots dodged bullets to evacuate the wounded, and field hospitals saved more lives than they lost.

Soldiers returning from war have seen the Veterans Administration change for the better in handling ancillary wounds of war. Vietnam Veterans had to battle for medical resources in their struggles against Agent Orange, which set a strong precedence for today's soldiers. And rightfully so!

The estimates of Post Traumatic Stress Disorders coming out of Iraq and Afghanistan, percentage wise, is the same as prior wars, but this time it will be easier for the soldiers of today to seek and get aid. Three to four-hundred thousand PTSD anticipated cases are sizeable but can be managed, especially if the government works on eliminating the stigma associated with mental care.

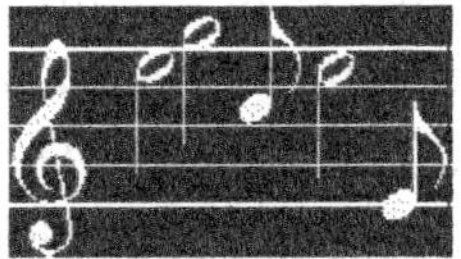

It's pretty as a daisy

Chapter X – On a Cold Metal Table

The Internet was fairly new when our chatgroup started and it took time for members to catch up to this technology. But when they did, things opened up and we all benefited from each other's communications, advice, and camaraderie. Everyone started to describe health symptoms which made it apparent Agent Orange diseases had become part of our lives. Some e-mailed they were suffering from diabetes, colon, testicle, and prostate cancers. Most of the Cavaliers had just turned 50ish and the prevalence of cancer was very high.

I was given marching orders from my wife to inform my doctor I was a Vietnam Veteran and he should be aware of AO and its consequences. I saluted her and contacted my doctor. It was the best order I was ever given and, thankfully, followed it to the letter.

My doctor found my Prostate Specific Antigen (PSA) was only at a 2.6 and he advised they don't become concerned until after it goes past four. However, he changed his mind when I mentioned Agent Orange and began to monitor it more often. Three months later the PSA had risen to 3.6 and he recommended further testing by a urologist.

The next test was completed two months later and again my PSA had risen; now it was at 4.3. The urologist completed a digital exam which showed an enlarged prostate. On September 22, 2000, biopsies were taken from both sides of the prostate showing stage II adenocarcinoma (malignant cancer). We celebrated my birthday that day thanking the heavens for an early detection.

Again, thanks to the Internet, we researched Prostate Cancer and the options available. Prostate cancer is a slow growing cancer most men experience later in life, usually in their 70s or 80s.

I visited with four urologists and several radiologists to get their views. We came to the conclusion that hormone treatments with radiation and seed implants had the least side affects and best suited our lifestyle. The hormone treatment was started first to reduce the size of the prostate. The rather sizeable needle injection in the lower abdomen was uncomfortable, but it did not compare to the incredible and insufferable hot-flashes.

The hot-flashes came along about every ten minutes making me sweat like I was in a steam bath. My wife and mother-in-law delighted in my discomfort and told me, "You're the only man who can truly understand women going through menopause." Their advice was to stick my head into the freezer since that worked very well for them. I did...and they were right!

Radiation treatment followed several months later and then 52 radioactive seed implants. The concern about the seed implants was setting off airport security while traveling. I envisioned being hauled away by the TSA for carrying radioactive isotopes, but fortunately that never happened.

E-mails did come in suggesting that in the dark my "rear end" would glow for at least a couple of months. Fellow Cavaliers are always up for harassing one of their own.

Radiation and Counseling

"Hello, Mr. Criser. How are you today?" said Howard in his usual courteous but hasty manner.

"Good, how are you? This is number five for me!" I responded, knowing that he was rushed to get me on the table to start this day's radiation session.

Howard, in his early thirties, was the radiation technician who very meticulously set up the Varian Technology Radiation machine so they could infuse 180 cGy external beam radiation into my prostate. The therapy was set up for 25 sessions; one each day for the next 20 weekdays.

"You're kind of young to have prostate cancer, aren't you?" Howard asked, feeling comfortable enough after five sessions to ask some personal questions.

"Yeah, they think prowling around in Agent Orange jungles for 14

months might have something to do with it," I replied like I had rehearsed that line, but it came to me for the first time. The impact of what I had just said hit Howard as much as it did me.

"Vietnam!" he stated with a sad undertone. *"I had an uncle who died there."*

"Yes, we lost a lot of good people over there...and now we are losing even more."

I didn't mean to sound so fatalistic; nevertheless, some of the statistics in 2001 had stated Vietnam Vets are being diagnosed with high rates of diabetes, bladder, colon, testicular, and prostate cancer. The report answered a lingering question for those who went in and out of the jungle filled with herbicides and defoliants.

"What kind of unit where you with?" he asked with greater curiosity.

"Remember the movie Apocalypse Now? That was the unit except that was around 1965. I was there in '69."

"Must have been pretty rough!" he commented, as he adjusted my position on the table.

"I was in C Troop, First of the Ninth, part of the 1st Air Cav. We were 60 miles northwest of Saigon near a town called Ben Hoa. My platoon was the ground reconnaissance and rescue part of a helicopter attack unit. I think we were lucky, because we only had two KIAs in our platoon while I was there."

"That was good. Did you go on a lot of missions?"

"We were out there on recon missions almost every day and we were out there day or night when we had a downed bird," I explained. He really was easy to talk to and seemed to be interested since he had a relative who never came back.

"Downed Bird?"

"Yes, a helicopter or plane that went down and we had to go out and rescue the crew, secure the craft or destroy it. We did that a bunch. The platoon was called the Blues, it was short for the Blue Annihilators."

"Ok, now hold still, breath normally and I will be right back," Howard said, as he left the room to start the radiation.

The subject we were talking about rang through my head when the high-pitched buzzing from the machine started, then stopped, moved 90 degrees and started one more time. That was the routine as the radiation beam was directed from four directions, each marked by tattoo like spots, ones I still have today.

"Mind if I ask you a personal question? And you don't have to answer if you don't feel like it," Howard said, with some hesitation as he walked back in.

To me, his tone sounded rather ominous and much more serious than anything we had talked about before. Previously we only told a joke or two and stayed pretty general in our chitchat.

"I heard you never saw the enemy. Did you ever come face-to-face with any of them?"

It was a peculiar question, because I was just thinking about an incident in July 1969, one that changed the war for me.

"Yes... Howard, as a matter of fact, I had such an encounter."

"Well, I have to take pictures of your prostate, so today we have time," he responded with his eyebrows raised and a certain amount of eagerness in his voice.

While the radiation tech made changes on the machine, I told him about the time we were moving slowly up a trail, which forked north and west. Our pointman went up the west fork, leaving our Vietnamese scout to watch the other trail. Just then the scout saw several North Vietnamese Army regulars walking straight toward us...about 30 feet away. They hadn't seen us.

When our scout saw them, he ran. He flew past me yelling something in his native tongue. The NVA pointman, hearing the commotion, stopped and started to raise his AK 47 he was carrying with both hands across his chest. We looked at each other and I could see he was as startled to see me, as I was to see him.

"OK, hold that thought, let me take the pictures," stated Howard, finishing his sentence on his way out the room, but letting me know, *"We'll have time to finish while the pictures develop."*

While he was taking the pictures, it gave me time to reflect on what happened on July 28th, 1969. Even after 30-years of being back in civilian clothes, telling stories brought up deeply disturbing emotions. It also caused tremendous anguish in the pit of the stomach and tears easily swelled in the corner of my eyes.

"Ok! Now you said you were staring an enemy in the face," Howard said, as he emerged from behind the heavy lead door, which protected him from the radiation.

The story I was about to tell him was one I had recently relayed to my wife, but never to a stranger. It was also the one event that made me look at war differently than ever before, as it brought to mind the consequences and effects war has on those waiting at home.

"We were inserted into a small LZ that had been scouted all morning and some fresh signs of the enemy showed up on trails just to the north," I began, took a deep breath and continued. *"This day we had two squads and a South Vietnamese scout who had been assigned to us a couple of weeks earlier. We neither trusted this scout, nor felt we needed him."*

I described, to the now seated technician, how the NVA and I looked at each other. He began raising his weapon to get it into firing position. The advantage of carrying a light M-16 with a pistol grip was it could be shot from the hip, something I had practiced continuously to the point where I could hit a two-inch wide road marker from 30-yards away. It was our habit to use tracer rounds, usually the first two in the magazine and then every fourth or fifth round, so we could see how accurate our shots were.

This is where all the training and practice took over. There was no thinking, no questions, just reaction. I flipped the safety to semi-automatic and with my first shot hit his AK causing it to discharge and jam, the second shot went straight into his jaw. He went down…and still, incredibly, crawled behind a large termite mound.

At the same time, Specialist 4 Mike Melton saw why our Vietnamese Scout was running, cold-cocked him with the butt of his M-60, and came forward to open fire on the rest of the NVA's. Melton finished off the others in quick succession.

Silence came as quickly as the bursts of gunfire that started the firefight. We checked for injured Blues and to see the condition of our scout. Thankfully, no one was hurt and the scout was slowly coming around. The silence was broken by the call on the radio from our scout bird that had heard the firefight.

"Blue, this is Red Robin, come in please."

"Red Robin, this is Blue-India...we made contact, please standby."

We called our situation to our cover birds and advised things were under control. Our pointman and his backup had made their way to the NVA KIAs, disarmed them, and began to search the bodies for information. The NVA pointman had made his way around the termite mound and tied a scarf around his wounded chin before he died.

"Howard, the worst possible thing happened," I explained. *"The guy had a picture in his pocket of what probably was his wife and she was holding a young baby girl." I lamented, took a shallow breath, and said, "I have never gotten over that."*

It wasn't easy to explain how before this event the enemy was just shadows in the bushes. Even when we had mopped up after a firefight and pulled bodies out of bunkers or bushes; they were still faceless enemies.

This was different. We all looked at the picture and without a word went on with the clean up and prepared to make our way back to the LZ. No one spoke about the picture...but I knew it had affected us all. Now, the enemy had a face; it was the face of a father, a husband, and someone's son.

"Even today I think that there is a thirty-some year old woman in North Vietnam who had lost her father that day," I said with a deep sigh.

"Wow! War is terrible, even for the survivors," commented Howard, and to break the moment said, *"We'll see you tomorrow."*

"Yup, same time, same place," I got in the habit of saying as I got off the cold and hard radiation table.

THE JULY 1969 OFFICIAL 1ST/9TH CAV REPORT STATED:

"*C troop supported Division Headquarters base defense with daily reconnaissance in AO Chief. During this period Troop C flew 370 missions. Significant actions during the month were the Aero-Rifle (Blues) Platoon had been inserted 18 times during this period, capturing many small ammunition caches. The rifle platoon also found one large food cache. The rifle platoon engaged the enemy two times... accounted for 3 enemies killed while on sweeping operation.*"

But look out Charlie's crazy He'll try to do you in
If you let him get under your skin
VI..ET..N..AM...VI..ET..N..AM
LATE AT NIGHT WHILE YOU'RE SLEEPING
CHARLIE CONG COMES A CREEPIN' ALL AROUND

Chapter XI – PTSD – A Chemical Change in the Brain

We all experienced exceptional "Traumatic Stress" when the "Twin Towers" fell, the Pentagon was attacked, and United Flight 93 crashed in the Pennsylvania field on September 11, 2001. And there are many who suffered PTSD from that horrific event. We all shared in the anger, frustration, and later depression when we heard the news over 3,000 were killed

However, those who buried their Vietnam Ghost more than likely had reoccurring PTSD or realized for the first time they are still influenced by the war. I know I did!

There are two additional dynamics that have surfaced since 9/11, making these emotions much deeper than might be expected; adding further anger, frustration, mistrust, and depression.

In a 2002 interview, published in The Wall Street Journal, former General Bui Tin who served on the general staff of the North Vietnamese Army and received the unconditional surrender of South Vietnam on April 30, 1975, confirmed the "American military victory" during the Tet 1968 offensive and that conditions for the North Vietnamese were much worse than anyone had expected.

Bui Tin stated, "*Our losses were staggering and a complete surprise. Giap (NVA Commanding General) later told me that Tet had been a military defeat, though we had gained political advantages when (President) Johnson agreed to negotiate and did not run for reelection. The second and third waves in May and September were, in retrospect, mistakes. Our forces in the South were nearly wiped out by all the fighting in 1968. It took us until 1971 to reestablish our presence but we had to use North Vietnamese troops as local guerrillas. If the American forces had not begun to withdraw under Nixon in 1969, they could have punished us severely. We suffered badly in 1968 and 1969 as it was."*

And on strategy he stated: "*If Johnson had granted Westmoreland's requests to enter Laos and block the Ho Chi Minh trail, Hanoi could not have won the war...*" (http:www.marine-family.org/vva/jane2.htm)

Victory was so close, yet so far!

Gulf of Tonkin Fiasco

A new factor uncovered in 2005 created an immeasurable credibility quagmire. Many still remember the Gulf of Tonkin incident where the North Vietnamese attacked the USS MADDOX and USS TURNER JOY in August 1964. There was a huge outcry about our Navy being attacked. The Media played up the fact and hyped everyone to a frenzied state to declare war and invade North Vietnam.

"How dare they attack this country!" we all thought.

The incident was responsible for Congress passing the "Gulf of Tonkin Resolution," which gave President Lyndon Johnson the authority to assist any country in Southeast Asia threatened by communism. It gave him the authority to escalate the war.

However, National Security Agency (NSA) documents released in 2005 under the Freedom of Information Act showed there was no such attack. The declassified report stated, "*It is not simply that there is a different story as to what happened; it is that no attack happened that night. [...] In truth, Hanoi's navy was engaged in nothing that night but the salvage of two of the boats damaged on 2 August.*"

More Vets Seek Help

About this time, the Veterans Administration began reporting a growing number of veterans walking into their healthcare facilities with signs of nervousness, depression, and thoughts of suicide. Many described increased nightmares and reoccurring dreams about the Southeast Asian war.

As the war in Afghanistan and then Iraq started taking its toll, more Vietnam Vets began showing signs of PTSD. For those of us in the 1st of the 9th Cavalry, we had additional stress and anxious times because our unit, as before, was right in the middle of the most dangerous actions in Iraq.

> The 1st of the 9th Cavalry is stationed in Iraq
>
> *"The mission of 1st Battalion, 9th Cavalry Regiment was to deploy, fight and win.... anytime the nation gives it the call.*
>
> *The Headhunters of the 1st Battalion, 9th Cavalry Regiment deployed to Iraq in early 2004.*
>
> *They were operating in a very complex environment as they conducted combat operations, assisted Iraqi institutions (Neighborhood councils, Iraqi National Guard, Iraqi police etc), and facilitated quality of life improvements for the Iraqi people.*
>
> *TF 1-9 CAV was located in downtown Baghdad, subordinate to 3rd BDE of the 1st CAV Division. Their area contained slums and lower to upper class neighborhoods. The dense urban terrain meant that the Headhunters had to do a whole lot of dismounted patrolling.*
>
> *The TF had been engaged in numerous combat actions. TF 1-9 CAV soldiers did very well against these attacks due to their high level of training, protective equipment, and courage under fire.*
>
> *Unfortunately, TF 1-9 CAV suffered some casualties while conducting the mission. By early July 2004 there were over 30 soldiers wounded and two killed."*
>
> (http://www.globalsecurity.org/military/agency/army/1-9cav.htm)

An e-mail we received from a fellow Cavalier made us feel proud, and unfortunately, distressed about the dangers our young soldiers are facing:

Date: Tue, 13 Nov 2007 11:02:42 -0800 (PST)
From: frank <frankjgam@ >
To: < trp9thcav@yahoo.com>
Subject: Re: Charlie Troop

Thank you sir for your support. Well it's been a long adventurous 14months here in Iraq for Charlie troop 1/9 Cav; we have done missions down south of our AO to all of northern Iraq, we are going home soon, twenty something days.

We have worked hard and accomplished allot, do I think we have made a change, I'm not too sure but that's not for me to decide, its for the people or Iraq. We fought well and charged hard and had fun in some of the worst places and turned them from nothing into something. we are currently living in Rubyia, Iraq right on the Syrian border, its been real fun us away from the rest of our squadron, us just relying on each other.

I would never trade one memory bad or good from all of this for anything in this world. to me you guys the original troopers, the hard "chargin" scouts of Vietnam and past generations you guys are my idols, my heroes no one had it as hard and as ruff as you guys did, and I respect and honor all of your sacrifices, so thank you, and thank you for your support.

RECON! SCOUTS OUT! SPC (P)FRANK J C TRP 1/9CAV 4BCT 1ST CAV DIV

It's very difficult knowing the 1/9th is again in heavy action. Moreover, many of us are part of an ever-growing group with relatives overseas. I have a nephew who served in Iraq. Our young heroes are facing the same dangers we did; as well as a possible future of coming home to problems you don't think about while ducking bullets. And as the war proceeds we receive news, which brings us all closer to the warriors of today:

To: "C Trp Group" ctrp9thcav@yahoogroups.com

Subject: Hundley's son dies in Iraq

Steve Hundley (Charlie Troop 1/9th '66-'67) lost his son to a roadside bomb in Iraq. Keep Steve and Marianne in your thought and prayers

To: "C Trp Group" ctrp9thcav@yahoogroups.com
From: "Jack Schwarz" <cavalier44@>
Date: Wed, 12 Dec 2007 13:56:33 –0500
Subject: Legacy Trooper Christmas

Folks,

Charlie Blue '70 has a son over in Iraq, how about taking a minute to send him Christmas greetings. Mikes letter follows:

Charlie Blue here,

I was hoping you could send my son Mark a Merry Christmas wish in Iraq. He is stationed and attached to the 1/9 Cav, amazing two generations of foolish youngsters in that coolest of Units. Anybody wishing to drop him a Cav Christmas wish can do so by e-mail at Mark@. I am sure he would love to here from those of us who did this Christmas stuff some thirty plus years ago.

The following communications had a very personal, negative, and confusing effect on me. I was incredibly honored to have numerous requests for the poem, "A Cavalier's Last Charge." Yet…I was heartbroken when I received these e-mails:

Date: Sun, 09 Jan 2005 13:12:21 –0600
From: "William H. Boudreau" <outpost@copper.net>
To: tlcriser@yahoo.com
Subject: Request "A Cavalier's Last Charge"

Tom

I came across a poem that you may have written a number of years ago - "A Cavalier's Last Charge". I am requesting your permission to use it on a Website dedicated to the Troopers of the 1st Cavalry that are killed in action in Iraq that is at URL http://www.first-team.us/fallen-defenders/

From: Jesse E Kitson, Sr
To: tlcriser@yahoo.com
Subject: Request permission to use your poem
Date: Tue, 30 Aug 2005 18:17:18 -0400

Mr. Criser,

I would like to use the poem that is on the 1st Cav Div web site for my best friend and Brother Ricky L Taylor who passed on Aug 23 and will be buried Sept 1. Ricky received the DFC for action with the 1st Cav on 21 Jul 1968.

Thank You, Jesse E. Kitson

From: "Phillip Leal" <armyscouttx@>
My name is SSG Leal, of B Troop 1/75th Cavalry Reg, 2BDE 502nd INF, 101st AirBorne Div (AASLT). This past year we lost two great NCO's SSG Bandenhil, and SGT Sakoda in Baghdad, Iraq. I just read your Poem and thought is would be very fitting to their memorial in our squadron headquarters.

SSG Leal, Felipe Jr.
B Troop 1-75th CAV.

As I mentioned, it was truly a mixed bag of emotions. Issues in the news about the war in Iraq and Afghanistan disturbed us all, but nothing serious at first. Discussions with our group showed frustration on everyone's part. We heard about one of the Army's choppers going down and the pilots assassinated and dragged through an Iraqi town. The messages read, *"Where were the Blues and other cover birds?"*

Many Cavaliers expressed their dissatisfaction and anger in e-mails. Some members displayed signs their frustration had taken on depression, nightmares, and headaches. Also, it was evident some experienced increased emotional numbness, withdrawal, and generally being unresponsive to things that used to interest them.

The feeling of unhappiness materialized slowly for me. When it did hit…it was evident something needed to be done. It was New Year's Eve 2004. Leslie and I were celebrating the evening on the Texas Treasure, a gambling ship out of Port Aransas, TX.

New Year's Eve parties have always been special for us; very dressy, and celebrated with a great deal of enjoyment. That was not the case this evening and my direct orders were to seek help ASAP at the VA.

I'm lucky to have a mate who is understanding, patient, and someone who believes in quickly seeking medical attention. Her persistent attitude, toward making my doctors aware of being a Vietnam Vet with a potential of contracting Agent Orange diseases, was responsible for the very early detection of my cancer.

Fortunately, I was scheduled for a cancer follow up visit the second week of the New Year. The triage nurse worked up a preliminary PTSD report. The symptoms she reviewed; sleeplessness, nightmares, depression, migraines, and thoughts of suicide, hit home. I never had thoughts of suicide, but all the others applied. My treatment consisted of visits with a psychiatrist and medication. The medication quickly changed my perspective and the sessions on the couch ended swiftly.

My doctor stated three to four Vietnam Vets were walking into the clinic daily with the same symptoms. According to the doctor, two factors were causing the trend: one, a sizable number of those suffering from Agent Orange disabilities are dying. And two, her opinion was the wars in Iraq and Afghanistan where bringing out hidden memories for Vietnam Vets which are causing delayed PTSD.

An e-mail from my Cavalier brother Walker Jones accurately summed up what most of us felt as the memories started pouring back…new brothers contacted us, and e-mails from young warriors about how to cope with life after being in the battlefield.

From: Walker Jones <cavalier@>
To: Tom Criser <tlcriser@yahoo.com>
Sent: Thursday, April 10, 2008 12:52:18 AM
Subject: [ctrp9thcav] Stop the Politics, or Die

Damn, Tom,

You know, I went for 25 years believing that I must have been the only Vietnam Vet that was not affected. When I decided to start finding out where my old buds ended up, and talking to them (and many more), I got blindsided by a f---n bus, right off the bat.

I cannot say that I have recovered sufficiently – most (of) the get-together/events have been ... really wonderful. But after several years after diving head first into this past, and helping so many others come out of their shells, I feel that I'm now withdrawing like a snail sprinkled with salt.

We never get over the hurt and the trauma. I'm just trying to sort out what my 3 nephews need from me. I now find myself needing to guide them through their Iraq/Afghanistan wars. They don't know what will hit them in 25 years. I feel so helpless. But the one thing that I always tell them is cling to your buds; they will be your best friends 20-30 years from now.

Best regards,

Walker

What is PTSD?

Post Traumatic Stress Disorder (PTSD): *an anxiety disorder that can develop after exposure to one or more terrifying events in which grave physical harm occurred or was threatened. It is a severe and ongoing emotional reaction to an extreme psychological trauma.*

This stressor may involve someone's actual death or a threat to the patient's or someone else's life, serious physical injury, or threat to physical and/ or psychological integrity, to a degree that usual psychological defenses are incapable of coping.

In some cases it can also be from profound psychological and emotional trauma, apart from any actual physical harm. Often, however, the two are combined.
(http://en.wikipedia.org/wiki/Post-raumatic_stress_disorder)

When the call comes that one of your own choppers just crashed and you're in the heart of the action, you don't have time to think. The call may come in the middle of the night. Your heart sinks when the rescue chopper approaches the barely visible LZ and all you can make out is the burning silhouette of the downed bird. Your training prevents you from becoming emotional, but your mind knows what lies ahead. Your only concern is to get there and hope you can find your brothers alive.

Frequently, no LZ is available and you have to repel 200 feet into the dark, forbidding jungle filled with all kinds of nasty unknowns. Your gut is all knotted and your head absolutely comprehends the bird was shot down and the enemy is almost certainly waiting for you. However, your body still follows what it was trained to do.

Can anything prepare you for seeing a co-pilot sitting against a tree with the pilot lying across his lap? Both KIAs! Or looking for the crewmember in the core of the burning remnants of what once was a dynamic fighting machine?

Is there any psyche that can endure the vision of using a long bamboo pole to push the door gunner's body out of the fire? Can your mind adjust to the fact that a few hours earlier you held a brief "Hi, how are you?" conversation with the now charred body in the bag?

How does a mind adjust to the horrors of war? Is it possible to come out "whole" from action where you see your friends die around you? Even worse than watching them die, is seeing them blown to pieces or burned past recognition. Scenes like that entrenches unimaginable stress on the brain.

There is no training…or past life experience, which can prepare you for the emotional chaos your mind goes through. Your mind forces the sights and sounds it just endured into an emotional closet that involuntarily opens later when you expect it the least.

Your conscious mind tries to shield you. However, the subconscious works on you continuously and the nightmares are your reminders. You feel off balance, migraines evolve, and realistic dreams cruelly startle you awake in the middle of the night. A feeling of hopelessness precludes you from being happy. Guilt sets in, fear follows, and suddenly you either shut off the emotional valve or your body just starts to shut down.

More than likely, that is the reason most Vietnam Vets buried their Ghosts into an impenetrable closet, fully intending never to open the door again. Coming home to cheerless crowds didn't help, but even cheers and parades don't wash the mind of visions no one should ever have to endure.

Nagging Thoughts Come Creepin'

Other aspects slowly work their way into your life. Some of the little things your mind keeps with you all the time. For many, it's a sound…like chopper blades flapping when they torque to slow the craft. Or it's unexpected loud noises. Many Vets recollect hitting the floor in the middle of a grocery store when glass shatters on the floor.

In our chatroom discussions, several cavaliers mentioned songs haunting them. Music we listened to while in Nam (The Chamber Brother's "Time Has Come") or songs we sang in training before going overseas just stay with you. Then, all of a sudden, your mind is singing the song for no reason. However, the effect is more sleepless nights, more depression, and a wonderment of "*will it ever stop?*"

During Basic and Advance Infantry Training we had a popular cadence song. A parity of The Coasters' 1959 hit "Poison Ivy." The song was popular when jogging for miles, because it easily converted to a topical subject.

You're gonna need an ocean of calamine lotion
You'll be scratching like a hound
The minute you start to mess around
Poi...son I...vy Poi...son I...vy
Late at night while you're sleeping
Poison Ivy comes a creepin all around

Our Version:

You're gonna need an ocean of Mosquito lotion
You'll be scratching like a hound
The minute you start to mess around
It's pretty as a daisy
But look out Charlie's crazy
He'll try to do you in
If you let him get under your skin
VI..ET..N..AM...VI..ET..N..AM
LATE AT NIGHT WHILE YOU'RE SLEEPING
CHARLIE CONG COMES A CREEPIN ALL AROUND

Those who experienced traumatic stress understand how little things pester away at you. Like this song has done for me since my return! I've heard scores of Vets indicate they experience the same thing with other triggers. It comes out of nowhere, happens at anytime, and always has the same PTSD affect.

The Stigma of PTSD

Unfortunately, the Baby-Boomer generation's mindset is entrenched in that any mental issues resulting from combat are considered a form of cowardice or weak moral character. The movie "Patton" with George C Scott exemplifies that attitude. The scene where General Patton slaps a soldier, hospitalized for shell shock, highlights the point.

Soldiers of World War II, Korea, and Vietnam would never admit to any kind of mental problems as a result of their combat experience because of the stigma. Research has shown career soldiers can kiss the future goodbye once their personnel file is branded with *"Medical treatment for psychological problems."*

The treatment for those warriors was Neolithic at best. Post Traumatic Stress Disorder wasn't even in our lexicon until the mid 1980's. There was very little help available and the treatment for these maladies was strictly psychological as the above definition suggests.

The Harvard Medical School's publication "Focus" covered PTSD in their March 2008 issue. Titled, "*PTSD: The Suffering Continues for Vets; The Vietnam War Put PTSD on the Map—It Has Not Gone Away.*"
(http://focus.hms.harvard.edu/2008/032108/public_health.shtml)

"*Despite advances, PTSD remains a legacy of Vietnam veterans. Almost 30 years after their return from Vietnam, 10 percent of veterans continue to experience severe PTSD symptoms, reports Karestan Koenen, HSPH assistant professor of society, human development, health, and epidemiology, and her co-authors in the*

February Journal of Traumatic Stress."

The report suggests long-term problems with PTSD. "*Our findings demonstrate exposure to combat during the Vietnam War continues to place veterans at risk for a wide variety of adverse psychological and social outcomes. Persisting PTSD was associated with worse family functioning, more smoking and drinking, less life satisfaction and happiness, more mental health service use, and more nonspecific health problems. About a quarter of a million Americans will develop PTSD at some point in their lives after being victimized or witnessing violence or other traumatic events. Rates are much higher in war veterans and people living in high-crime areas.*

Symptoms can develop long after the event and usually include recurrent terrifying recollections of the trauma. Sufferers typically avoid situations and people who trigger the memories and often have debilitating anxiety, irritability, insomnia and other signs of stress.

Though preliminary, the study provides needed insight into a condition expected to hit rising numbers of veterans returning from Afghanistan and Iraq, said Dr. Thomas Insel, director of the National Institute of Mental Health."

Additionally, the article states there are no time limits on when PTSD shows up or how long it might last. The report also maintains:

"*...trends in VA treatment of PTSD in the journal Health Affairs seems to confirm their findings. From 1997 to 2005, mental-health-service use among younger veterans of the Persian Gulf era has greatly increased, especially in the last five years and among younger*

Vets. Veterans from earlier service eras surprised researchers with a five-fold increase in use, especially among Vietnam Vets with PTSD. The system is straining at the seams, the researchers observed."

Post Traumatic Stress Disorder for all veterans is now getting the attention from the media, and because of an election year, lots of political play. A recent Associated Press headline read, "*22,000 Vets call suicide hot line.*" The subheading was, "*Post-Traumatic Stress Disorder Still Prevalent.*"

The article discussed how in the first year of operation the VA hotline has received "*As many as 250 calls per day – double the average number calling when it began.*"

Additionally, the VA estimates in excess of 6,000 veterans commit suicide each year and veterans are twice as likely to take their life as non-veterans. The data suggest the calls are evenly divided between Iraqi, Afghanistan, and Vietnam veterans. (Caller Times –AP release, Euphrat, K. July 28, 2008)

A friend, who is aware that I'm working on this project, sent me a very noteworthy article from the Washington Post: "Treating Wounds You Can't See" June 29, 2008, by Linda Blum, a clinical psychologist in New Jersey.

(www.washingtonpost.com/wp-dyn/content/article/2008/06/27/AR2008062702863.htm)

The article reviews many factors and effects PTSD will have on those returning from Iraq and Afghanistan. It also reviews VA cases Dr. Blum handled and those soldiers' reaction to the battlefield trauma. Her closing comments were very insightful and worth repeating.

"The brain can't just change the channel, like a TV remote, I tell them. Why do people expect their brains to be endlessly pliable, to be able to heal

rapidly and perfectly after such trauma? Perhaps it's because a mental injury is invisible, which encourages the fantasy that it will go away overnight. But the change in emotional reactions and behavior cuts so close to the sense of self. For my patients, the trauma isn't something that happens to you. It is you."

What struck me about the article was before my treatment I would connect to those individuals and experience stress and depression. Now, I look at those young soldiers and empathize, but I also feel they should know there is a time where recovery is complete enough to function and live happily ever after.

I e-mailed Dr. Blum and received a wonderful response:

Date: Sun, 29 Jun 2008 16:03:50 -0600
From: tlcriser@yahoo.com
To: "LBlum" <lfblum@verizon.net>
Subject: Re: Treating Wounds You Can't See -- PTSD

Tom Criser wrote:

Thanks for your work with our soldiers. As a Vietnam Vet who put his war into a closet for 30 years, like most, PTSD is something that can have a significant impact even now.

However, what I wanted to let you know is through the Internet, quite a few members of my unit have worked out problems and now, after 10 years, feel pretty good. What we have found to be noteworthy in finding an answer to our PTSD, (as you said, "the trauma isn't something that happens to you. It is you.") is to help others find themselves.

For us, the communications through the Internet has made us all feel closer together and that we are not alone. We share stories of the same events and for us who intentionally tried to forget most things about Nam, it has made us all stronger to deal with the chemical changes our brains went through.

With the support of knowledgeable and caring friends, family members, and healthcare professionals there can be a satisfactory resolution to Post Traumatic Stress Disorder.

Thanks, Cheers, Tom

Date: Mon, 07 Jul 2008 13:08:30 -0400
From: "LBlum" <lfblum@verizon.net>
To: tlcriser@yahoo.com
Subject: Re: Treating Wounds You Can't See -- PTSD

Thank you for your letter. I'm delighted to know that you've been able to utilize the internet to connect with members of your unit; you seem to have developed an informal therapy group. It also sounds as if you've been able to extract some meaning and insight from your Vietnam experience, and, of course, it's wonderful if something positive can be reaped from much suffering. Congratulations on your recovery, and all the best.

Linda Blum

Official Urged Fewer Diagnoses of PTSD

Regrettably, there are other articles which raise serious integrity issues with how the Veteran's Administration operates:

"*Official Urged Fewer Diagnoses of PTSD*," read one Washington Post headline. (Friday, May 16, 2008: A02. Lee, C. Washington Post Staff Writer).

The basics of the article are a VA psychologist's e-mail to mental-health specialists and social workers at the Department of Veterans Affairs' Center in Temple, Texas. The controversy is whether the VA staff is limited in the time they spend in diagnoses and should consider using the less severe Adjustment disorder.

The e-mail reads, "(VA staff members) *...really don't...have time to do the extensive testing that should be done to determine PTSD.*" The diagnosis of Adjustment Disorder does not qualify for payments to the veterans, even though it does provide for medical treatment.

"*Many veterans believe that the government just doesn't want to pay out disability that comes along with PTSD diagnosis, and this revelation will not allay their concerns,*" stated a watchdog group chairman. (VoteVets.org).

Articles like that sells newspapers. I can only speak to my experience with the VA and its healthcare system. Yes, there are bureaucratic policies which can drive you up a wall. However, overall I have had a very satisfactory experience with the system and the agency has been more than fair in their dealings with me.

I know many Vets have had to fight for every little thing and have initially been denied benefits. Sadly, inefficient bureaucracy is a failing in any organization; especially one as enormous as the VA Healthcare System.

Brothers Find Some Answers

The benefits of our 1/9th chatroom are many. None, however, is as important as talking with fellow soldiers who where there with you. Those who understand what it took to be at war and the return home. Opening up the closet and letting The Ghost out slowly is therapeutic, especially when you share it with those allies.

Some brothers open up quite readily and you can see the relief they have found. Others still struggle and continue to work on finding their own resolution. The following e-mail clearly summarizes the numerous e-mails we received in the last few years:

To:ctrp9thcav@yahoogroups.com
From: "mike1734" <mike1734@>
Date:Fri, 09 Jan 2004 02:13:48 -0000
Subject:[ctrp9thcav] Thank You

While I realize that I do not post a lot or do the chat thing I must tell all of you Thank You a very great deal. Since my wife found your web site a while ago and I read most of your postings a change has slowly come over me. Recently over the holidays my daughter said to me something like this "Dad, we thought that were a little wacko, checking out your Vietnam compatriots, but all of us are noticed that you are not so angry anymore" Well it floored me until I started to realize the healing that seems to have been going on slowly but surely. Again Thanks to all of you, from my family. Seems a damn shame it took so long though.
Thanks again, Mike

A Chemical Change in the Brain

Over the last 8 years a great deal of advancement in medicine and mental health has shown PTSD is a real physical affliction that must be treated like war related wounds that bleed. This new approach advocates that PTSD is… "***A brain disorder. It is not caused by a moral weakness or a character flaw.***"

That revelation is spelled out in an article of the National Institute of Health's, "*News in Health*." In the August 2008 issue, the article states, "*There are well-documented changes in the function and structure of the brain regions mediating fear and memory in PTSD… New strategies for developing better PTSD treatments will come from a better understanding of the chemical and structural changes in the brain that are associated with PTSD. Currently, NIH is funding several brain imaging studies to gain insight into the changes that take place in the brain during PTSD.*"
(www.newsinhealth.nih.gov)

A 2008 article "*The Brain: Brain Chemistry, and PTSD*" by W.E. Krill, Jr. MSPC, states:

"***PTSD is all about brain chemistry and what happens to the brain during and immediately after the critical, and traumatic incident. Essentially, the chemicals that flood the brain during the trauma do so in order to help the person to survive the event, either by running away, or fighting furiously.***

A third option, to submit to the trauma also has brain chemistry implications. In some individuals, once the brain goes through this chemical 'rewiring' to survive the trauma, the wiring stays that way."

The last statement is probably the most important sentence in this entire book and worth repeating, "***Once the brain goes through this chemical 'rewiring' to survive the trauma, the wiring stays that way.***"

What I get out of this statement is when we watch a horror flick, like "Friday the 13th" or "Halloween", our brain's chemicals react during the scary scene putting us in a fight or flight mode. The chemicals that wired our brain into that mode stops once you feel safe. Then…the brain quickly rewires.

However, during **severe** trauma, the chemicals are so strong the brain cells stay in an open mode. Because the wiring remains open, the trauma is repeatedly experienced during stress. Severe trauma increases the frequency of the flashbacks, intensifies the nightmares, and deepens the depression.

The article also states, "***Stress of a traumatic type may shrink the hippocampus (medial temporal lobe), and actually kill neurons there, as well as drastically slow down the growth of the new neurons.***

In addition to this startling finding, the 'wiring' of the brain's petrochemical system become over sensitized, and this results in the symptoms commonly seen in PTSD."

In plain language, this affects the brain's ability to control emotions and, at times, physical reactions such as trembling hands and quivering knees.

Also, "The chemical releases of noradrenalin, dopamine, serotonin, insulin, and cortisol; all play a complex part in PTSD and why it is so difficult to find effective medication to those who suffer. It suggests why PTSD affects sleep and being calm enough or alert enough to carry out every day tasks." (http://hubpages.com/hub/the-brain)

Genetic Research Started

Genetic research currently is being conducted and how a stress related gene may make some people more susceptible to this ailment as the following article advocates:

Post Traumatic Stress Gene ID'd, Lindsey Tanner, Associated Press

March 18, 2008 -- Cutting-edge new research helps answer the puzzling question of why post-traumatic stress doesn't happen to everyone who endures horrible trauma. The study of 900 adults is among the first to show that genes can be influenced by outside, non-genetic factors to trigger signs of post-traumatic stress disorder, or PTSD.

"The study is groundbreaking. The larger of just two reports to show molecular evidence of a gene-environment influence on PTSD," said Karestan

Koenen, a Harvard psychologist doing similar research. "We have known for over a decade, from twin studies, that genetic factors play a role in vulnerability to developing PTSD, but have had little success in identifying specific genetic variants that increase risk of the disorder," Koenen said.

"The results suggest...to outside influences that can shape the developing stress-response system," said Emory University researcher and study co-author Dr. Kerry Ressler.

The study appears in the *Journal of the American Medical Association*. Ressler noted that there are likely many other gene variants that contribute to risks for PTSD and others may be more strongly linked to the disorder than the ones the researchers focused on. (http://dsc.discovery.com/news/2008/03/18/post-traumatic-gene-print.html)

A Change in Perspective

Many Vets expressed their concerns about PTSD this way. "*I'm not a hero, but I'm also not a coward. To admit to Post Traumatic Stress Disorder is saying I can't handle combat, I can't handle the stress, and therefore...I am a coward.*"

I concurred with that 100 percent. I'm the son of a proud Air Force Colonel and my uncle was a "stolz" storm-trooper in the German Army. Our family has strong feelings that serving your country is an honor, one worth dying for.

However, like most Vietnam Vets, we lived in denial because of "cowardice" stigma. That thought pattern entrenched itself over 30 years and one would think it would be that way forever. Not so! When I was told PTSD had nothing to do with moral character or cowardice, I readily accepted that I have been suffering from this condition for a long time.

When I speak with fellow Vets, especially the ones from the current wars, I emphasize PTSD is an unseen wound requiring the same care as those that bleed. In almost every case, the response is one of relief, increased open communications, and a greater willingness to accept PTSD is part of their life. We all now approach the unseen wounds with a more positive, resolute, and proactive attitude.

Chapter XII – I Think I'm OK Now!

While in the midst of writing this book, I e-mailed my former 1st of the 9th CO Bob Tredway, which revealed a great deal about current feelings of The Ghost in my Closet.

Wed, 18 Jun 2008 07:27:27 -0700 (PDT)
From: "Tom Criser" <tlcriser@yahoo.com>
Subject: updating some memories
To: Robert Tredway"
Bob, I was just looking at some e-mails from Claude Newby and the mission we had Oct 30, 1969. The Blues lost Roger Carroll that day on a LRRP extraction. I remember your bird coming in and dumping some ammo for us while in the air. The LZ was too hot and you hovered about 30 feet above us. I heard that you took some rounds while doing that. Is my memory off? I know we ended up spending the night out there. How is your memory on that?
Thanks, Tom

Thur, 19 Jun 2008 08:27:27 -0700 (EDT)
From: Robert Tredway
Subject: updating some memories
To: "Tom Criser" <tlcriser@yahoo.com>

Tom, Wow. How do you remember those details? The facts are as you have stated. We had to hover high as the clearing was not big enough for the rotors to clear. We had gone to the 7th Cav firebase and "borrowed" an M-60 and assorted ammo, put it in a sling and returned to deliver the goodies. After the sling was emptied we backhauled the body to the 7th Cav firebase and arranged for the lift of a rifle company to be put in a clearing about 1500 meters from your location. We departed the AO after everyone knew where everyone else was located. Nice to hear from you. Cheers, Bob

Fri, 20 Jun 2008 09:38:42 -0700 (PDT)
From: "Tom Criser" <tlcriser@yahoo.com>
Subject: updating some memories
To: Robert Tredway"

Bob, memory is working its way back, which is making me feel much better. I have come to a resolution that many good things came from our war and now more of the country is recognizing that aspect. I'm hoping we can pass it on to the heroes of today and make their coming home much easier.

Later, T

When I wrote the words, "M*emory is working its way back, which is making me feel much better,*" I sat back and thought about what I had written. Yes, my memory was coming back with much more detail and what surprised me is my passion in those memories was not bundled up like before.

Most Vets will tell you their feelings get the best of them when they start opening their closet that has held their traumatic memories for so long. Just like the response from Forrest and the comments he made to his friends: (*Even now as I pause to read what I've written to you I choke and tear up with emotion recalling those days so long ago filled with adventure, death, thrill, and fear)*

The tears and choked emotions have always been part of thinking back. Researching this book, and the years of communicating with fellow Cavaliers, is having a positive effect and giving us a bright light at the end of the PTSD tunnel.

Shortly after the e-mails with Bob, I went to visit my daughter, her husband, and my seven-month-old grandson in the Washington, DC area. My original trip was getting there Thursday and returning Tuesday. But there was a thunderstorm in my layover city, Dallas, and the flight was cancelled. So, I rescheduled.

However, the airline mixed up my dates and I ended up going from Friday to the following Saturday. I had everything packed for a four-day trip, including my medications. Since 2003 my VA doctor has prescribed 20 mg of Citalopram Hydrobromide for mood. It was switched to 40 mg in 2005.

When I arrived at my daughters, I realized I didn't have enough pills so I cut the dosage in half. Even then, I was still short by two days. The lower dosage showed in my symptoms from the second day with a migraine lasting two days.

The last two days of my visit I felt extremely off balance and the back of my legs and head had a strange tingle. The physical effect of the reduced medication was clear. However, I did notice my mood was still good. There was no depression, no negative thoughts, and I really felt like I was making a breakthrough. I felt good!

The following weekend we sailed from North Padre Island to Ingleside, Texas for the annual "Bastille Day" celebration held at the Bahia Marina. It was our first time and we wondered why anyone would want to celebrate Bastille Day. It became pretty evident the reason was to have a party weekend and any excuse would do. The French Holiday seemed appropriate, because the event occurred around July 14th each year. It was a surprise how many boats and people showed up; over 40 sailboats with a couple hundred people. The major part of the event was a Blue Plate dinner and after dark the burning of a replica of the Bastille Prison while fireworks went off.

Watching fireworks have always been a major problem. For weeks I would have restless nights and Leslie would have to guard against accidentally being kicked. So, now that I began to feel better about having PTSD, we decided this was going to be a test to see how I would react. A test I was now ready and willing to take.

Saturday evening came along with people milling around finding a place to sit and eating an excellent dinner. We chose a table where three other people were already seated, a local realtor and a couple who came down from Fort Worth.

The thing I am still getting used to about Texas is how friendly and open the people are. When you meet people it usually makes for lengthy and laid-back discussions. It's not unusual to say hello and end up with that person's life history before the conversation ends.

Our discussion worked its way around the current war and serving in the military. The gentleman at our table stated proudly he was in the 1st Cav in 1968.

"Wow...A fellow Cavalier!" I said.

"Yes, 'Alpha' Troop, 1st of the 9th."

"Charlie Troop, 1969...70," I responded with excited interest.

"It's a small world!" we both stated in unison and instantly bonded.

The show started with two men in a canoe rowing the Bastille out about 40 feet from shore. They put stakes in the shallow bay water to hold the Bastille in one place. The winds didn't cooperate and they struggled with it for a good 20 minutes. The crew rowed back about halfway when the wind blew the Bastille away from shore. They feverishly rowed to catch it and spent another ten minutes putting it back. This happened twice before one of them got out of the canoe and pushed the stakes deeper to hold the model.

That's when the French jokes started:

"Guess they must be French, planning things out well in advance, like 10 seconds!" someone yelled.

"No, they can't be French, they know how to row a boat," another shouted from the laughing crowd.

"Of course, they're French, one has abandoned the ship."

The yelling now took on a more *"Let's make fun of the French"* demeanor.

The antics of lighting of the fireworks added more fuel to the laughter. Once the Bastille was secured, the men rowed back to shore, picked up a can of gasoline, and rowed back out for the fifth time.

"Knowing the French, I bet they forgot the matches!" my fellow Cavalier bellowed.

"Do the French know how to use matches?" someone hollered,

"No, they still rub two sticks together!" was the response.

The two men poured the gas on the cardboard model, argued for a minute, and then rowed back.

"See, they did forget the matches," a bunch yelled and the laughter now was infectious. The alleged French sailors rowed out once more…with the matches. The first rocket took some time to light and when it did go off, it headed skyward for a split-second. Then it made this dying duck sound and fizzled into the water.

"Isn't that how the French signal to surrender?" came from the crowd as a last stab.

Needless to say, the fireworks did manage to go off, 45 minutes late, and it was quite a show. The fire soon began to engulf the Bastille to roars of applause and cheers.

Even though I felt ready for the test, I took my doctors recommendation of taking an additional 20 milligrams of my "mood" prescription. The medication worked very well. Instead of nightmares for that night, I just had dreams which really were not disturbing. It was still about war, but more like seeing it in a movie theater. And very importantly, there were no additional sleepless nights. I really wish I had thought of the increased medication years ago; it truly might have made life a lot easier and safer for my wife.

The next incident was another very positive step that has made me feel much better about this unseen wound. Leslie and I love to watch movies. When we find one we both like, we will watch it again and again.

Leslie is fortunate, because she can put her brain into "auto-erase" for TV shows and movies. She can watch the same show over and over and she feels like it's the first time. *"I don't remember seeing this part?"* she always says, when it is the same thing we have already seen.

After watching Tiger Woods win the 2008 U.S. Open at Torrey Pines on a bum knee, I decided we should watch a golf movie. I picked the movie "The Legend of Bagger Vance," starring Will Smith, Matt Damon, and Jack Lemon. Yes, the gentleman I met while in High School some 40 years ago. It was his last role…he passed away June 27, 2001.

As we watched the movie, I noticed the considerably graphic World War I battle scene had minimal affect on me. Before…I always had to look away…my stomach would tighten…and I could feel my pulse accelerate. The scene of soldiers charging into blazing guns and getting blown away by explosions always had an impact and it took a while before I could get back into the lightheartedness of the film. Not this time. This time I enjoyed the movie all the way through. It made me think of why there was such a difference and that for the first time I realized what the real plot was.

"So, tell me what this movie was all about?" I asked Leslie.

"It's about a golf match between Bobby Jones, Walter Hagen, and

Rannudolf Junuh in the 1930's."

"What was the plot?" I asked.

"Junuh lost his golf swing and Bagger helped him find it."

"What made him lose his swing?"

"World War I and his entire platoon being killed," she said, as her eyes opened wide. *"He suffered from PTSD! That's right...I never thought of that!"*

"Neither had I!" I told her.

We had watched this movie over a dozen times and really never understood that point. But it was clear he suffered from shell shock or Post Traumatic Stress Disorder.

"Do you think Bagger was a real person? I mean, in the end he shows up still looking young and waving to Jack Lemon's character that now is old," she asked.

"Yeah, makes you wonder what Bagger represented?" I said, mulling that thought in my mind. I deliberated about how Junuh has a breakdown while trying to hit his ball in the woods. He momentarily relives the traumatic battle...his hands and knees shake and he says, *"I can't do this."*

"*Yes, you can. It's time you laid this down to rest*!" Bagger says. *"It's not your fault...and you've carried this burden long enough."*

Bagger Vance was telling this soldier to crack open his nailed-up closet. Was Bagger The Ghost in Junuh's closet?

The movie has a happy ending, Junuh gets the girl, the match ends in a draw, and you go away with a good feeling. They say movies imitate life... and life, at times, imitates the movies.

My fellow Cavaliers, my family, and my friends are my Bagger Vance. They helped me discover "The Ghost in my Orange Closet" is not something I should fear...nor should memories of a traumatic experience ever be locked in a closet. Yes, locking memories away seems to be the easy path to take, but it's not. If anything, it makes the road to recovery so much longer.

What I learned over the last eight years is open communications with friendly ears is vital. Quickly accepting you have the "unseen wound" is imperative. And believing…no!...being convinced that recovery from Post Traumatic Stress Disorder is absolute.

NOT THE END! As this book went to print, our chatgroup received the following e-mail:

(ctrp9thcav) Peter Guthrie
Monday, September 15, 2008 3:54 PM
From: "Patbnamin" <pcbnamin@>
To: ctrp9thcav@yahoo.com

After more than three years of looking, I finally found 1LT Peter Guthrie (Blue 68-69). I have made numerous phone calls and sent out numerous emails to every Peter Guthrie I could find.

I even zeroed in on as many Peter G. Guthries as I could. Two nights ago I left a message on an answering machine and asked if this was the right Peter Guthrie to please call me.

I just received his call. I have sent him this website. He wants to hear from everyone who wants to talk to him. He will not be able to make it to this years reunion but I doubt seriously if he will miss too many from here on.

Pat

The search continues for more Veterans to come forward
so they can step up and strive to expel their
"Ghost in the Orange Closet."